The Night Thoreau Spent in Jail

The Night Thoreau
Spent in Jail

A play by
Jerome Lawrence and Robert E. Lee

Hill and Wang
A division of Farrar, Straus and Giroux
New York

Hill and Wang
A division of Farrar, Straus and Giroux
18 West 18th Street, New York 10011

Printed in the United States of America
Published in 1971 by Hill and Wang
First paperback edition, 2001

Library of Congress Card Number: 70-148234
ISBN 0-8090-1223-5 (pbk.)

www.fsgbooks.com

20

The Now Thoreau

THE MAN imprisoned in our play belongs more to the moment than to
the age in which he lived.

For more than a century, Henry David Thoreau was dismissed as a
gifted weirdo. Only a rebel like Emerson's handyman would dare to
question the benefits of technology! Why, it is obvious to any educated
mind that technological advancement and progress are synonymous.
To create a better world, all we have to do is make things bigger,
faster, stronger, or cheaper.

But materialism is not the way.

THOREAU KNEW THAT.

He smelled the smog before we saw it.

It smarted his soul before it smarted our eyes.

He spoke out; but in those television-less days men were slow to
listen. He sang out in nonviolent defiance, but how few men since
could carry the tune: Gandhi, Count Tolstoi, Martin Luther King.

It was the material-mindedness of his government which drove the
mystic Thoreau to the shores of Walden. His outrage is closely akin
to the anger of many young people today. Young Thoreau was disgusted by the lies and confusion which clouded the bloody conflict
with a smaller nation, Mexico.

The President of the United States (James Polk) had made a pre-
tense of trying to settle differences at the conference table. Then, without a declaration of war or Congressional approval, U.S. forces plunged
into Mexico. An inaccurate and incomplete report from the President
(which has been lamely explained by the lack of electrical communica-
tion) brought authorization from Congress.

Hawks and white supremacists of the day cheered. But the in-
tellectual community gasped in horror.

The text of the play contains a denunciation of the war actually made by a young Whig Congressman from Illinois—who was not re-elected because of his stand, but who later became the first Republican President of the United States.

American secret agents smuggled in a puppet president from Havana. Overwhelmed by U.S. armor, the Mexicans resisted all the way to the gates of their capital, which fell only when their ammunition ran out. On the side of the invaders, there was hot friction between secret envoys from the White House, an alarmed Congress, and the ambitious military leaders—two of whom became Presidents of the United States and one of the Confederacy.

A captain in the army of General Winfield Scott reported that the American troops acted like savages. They shot noncombatants on trivial pretexts. "Their conduct toward the poor inhabitants has been horrible and their coming is dreaded like death in every village."

Another eyewitness, Ulysses S. Grant, wrote in his memoirs: "I do not think there was ever a more wicked war than that waged by the United States on Mexico. I thought so at the time, when I was a youngster, only I had not the moral courage to resign." Grant had the option of resignation, which has not been granted to youngsters of later wars.

According to Santayana, "Those who do not remember the past are condemned to relive it." Perhaps this play will jog our memories as we relive the poetic protest of one of America's freest men.

Time is awash in this jail cell. We are not trapped in happenings past. The explosive spirit of Thoreau leaps across the years, addressing with power and clarity the perils of his own time and, prophetically, of ours as well.

Thoreau is a fascinating paradox:

A man who was—and is.

A self-effacing giant.

A wit who rarely laughed.

A man who loved so deeply and completely that he seemed, sometimes, not to have loved at all.

JEROME LAWRENCE
ROBERT E. LEE

vi

The Night Thoreau Spent in Jail was presented first in 154 different productions by resident, community, and university theatres throughout the United States, through The American Playwrights Theatre. The pilot production was presented at the Ohio State University, Columbus, Ohio, as the university's centennial play, on April 21, 1970. Dr. Roy Bowen directed. The cast was as follows:

WALDO	Donald Mauck
LYDIAN	Dorothy Laming
MOTHER	Irene Martin
HENRY	David Ayers
JOHN	Anthony B. Schmitt
BAILEY	Burton Russell
BALL	John W. Toth
ELLEN	Bronwynn Hopton
SAM	Al Converse
EDWARD	Michael David Ayers
WILLIAMS	Gary Easterling
PASSER-BY	Donald Shandler
DRUNK	Corwin Georges
FARMER	Bruce Vilanch
WOMAN	Jerri Aberman
TOWNSPEOPLE	Floyd E. Hughes III
	Richard Pierce
	Evy Steffens
	Ann Goldman
	Sandra Kalenik
	Dorothy Konrad
	Robert Segall

Scene Design by Russell T. Hastings
Costume Design by David L. Chappell
Lighting Design by W. Alan Kirk
Original Music by J. A. Huff
Percussion Music by Charles Spohn
War Scene staged by Lynn Dally

The initial production mating professional and academic theatre took place at UCLA during summer and fall of 1970. Guy Stockwell starred as Henry, with True Boardman as Waldo. Robert E. Lee directed.

Act One

If a man does not keep pace with his companions, perhaps it is because he hears a different drummer. Let him step to the music which he hears, however measured, or far away.

HENRY DAVID THOREAU

(*Center is the skeletal suggestion of a prison cell: two crude cots, a chair, a wooden box which serves as a clothes locker. An imaginary window downstage looks out on Concord Square.*

A Thrust extends forward, not part of the cell—nor are the playing areas at either side. The cell itself is raked. The cell door, imaginary, is upstage center.

Surrounding the cell is the sky over Concord. There are night bird sounds, distant. Two men lie on the cots, motionless. Striped moonlight through the prison bars falls across HENRY, *but the man on the other cot is in shadow.*

Time and space are awash here.

Into a weak winter light, unrelated to the cell, an old man enters on the arm of his wife. He walks with studied erectness, using an umbrella as a cane. The wife is handsomely patrician. The old man has a shawl over his shoulders, a muffler around his neck. He stops.)

WALDO (*Suddenly, as if somebody had stolen his wallet.*)
What was his name?

LYDIAN
Whose name?

WALDO
I've forgotten the name of my best friend!

LYDIAN
Did you ever have a best friend?

WALDO
The boy. Who put the gloves on the chickens.

LYDIAN
Henry?

WALDO (*Vaguely.*)
I keep thinking his name was David.

(*Light strikes* HENRY'S MOTHER *as she comes into another area, also*

3

apart from the cell. She is distressed, piling disheveled hair onto the top of her head.)

MOTHER

David Henry! What have you gone and done?

(HENRY *rises on the cot. He is 29, clean-shaven, with liquid eyes. His clothes are simple, the colors of the forest. This is a young man—with a knife-like humor, fierce conviction and devastating individuality.*)

HENRY

I have not gone and done anything, Mother. I have gone and *not* done something. Which very much needed the *not* doing.

MOTHER

Oh, good heavens!

(*Calling off stage.*)

Louisa! David Henry's gone and *not* done something again.

HENRY (*Correcting her.*)

Henry David.

MOTHER

David Henry, you're being strange again.

WALDO (*Distantly.*)

He was strange. I almost understood him.

LYDIAN

Sometimes.

MOTHER

Sometimes I don't know who you are.

HENRY

I'm myself, Mother.

(*He lifts himself and sits on the edge of the cot.*)

If I'm not, who will be?

MOTHER

When you're baptized, they tell you who you are.

HENRY

I wasn't listening.

MOTHER

At the christening you didn't cry once, not once. Reverend Ripley said how remarkable it was for a baby not to cry at a christening.

4

HENRY

You think I knew what they were doing to me?

MOTHER

I suppose not.

HENRY

That's why I didn't cry.

WALDO

He was the saddest happy man I ever knew.

LYDIAN

The happiest sad man, I think.

WALDO

He worked on Sundays, and took the rest of the week off.
(*Staring at his umbrella, puzzled.*)
Who's this?

LYDIAN

It's your umbrella.

WALDO

Oh, yes.
(*He studies the umbrella affectionately, as if it were a lost old friend.*)
Yes, my . . . uh . . . my . . .
(*But again he's lost the name.*)
Yes.
(LYDIAN *helps the vague* WALDO *off, as the lights fall away on them.*)

MOTHER

I wouldn't mind your being peculiar. But do you have to *work* at it so hard, David Henry?

HENRY

Henry David.

MOTHER

Getting everything backward. How did you learn your letters?

HENRY

Must the alphabet begin with A? (*He stands.*) Why not with Z? Z is a very sociable letter. Like the path of a man wandering in the woods. A is braced and solid. A is a house. I prefer Z. Z-Y-X-W-V-U-T-S——
(*He makes a zig-zag course out of the cell into the thrust area.*)

5

MOTHER

Oh, dear——!

HENRY

Or mix them up. Start with H. Start with Q.

(WALDO, *younger and straighter, has moved to a lectern where the light makes his face glow with an inner radiance. He is at the climax of an address.*)

WALDO (*Projecting.*)

Cast Conformity behind you.

(HENRY *sees* WALDO, *and sinks to the floor, sitting squat-legged as a youthful admirer at the feet of an idol.*)

HENRY (*As if memorizing a Commandment.*)

"Cast . . . Conformity . . . Behind You . . . !"

(JOHN *enters, stands beside his disturbed* MOTHER. *Both look at* HENRY, *as he sits in a Yoga-esque fixation, staring up into empty air.* JOHN *is taller than his brother—affable, more extroverted.* JOHN *moves smoothly, easily, in contrast to the explosively erratic movements of his younger brother.*)

MOTHER

You know what David Henry's trouble is, John?

JOHN

What?

MOTHER

He keeps casting conformity behind him!

JOHN (*Shrugging.*)

What the hell, he's been to Harvard.

MOTHER (*Offended.*)

Never say——

JOHN

Harvard? I'm sorry, Mother, I'll never say it again.

(MOTHER *goes off, and* JOHN *saunters toward his brother, who still sits transfixed. He looks at* HENRY *with some amusement.*)

Now here's a rare specimen——

WALDO

(*The vital glow still upon his face.*)

There is an infinitude in the private man! If a single man plants him-

6

self indomitably on his instincts, and there abide, the huge world will come round to him . . .

(*The light falls away on* WALDO *as he goes off. The light intensifies on* HENRY *and* JOHN—*the amber of sunny fields.*)

HENRY (*Still squatting; to himself.*)
. . . and there abide!

(JOHN *circles* HENRY *playfully, as if examining a specimen.*)

JOHN
Hm! Is this one wild or tame? Wild, I think. Known to haunt the woods and ponds. Dull plumage. But a wise bird. Americanus something-or-other. I have it! It is the species—BROTHER!!!

(*This joshing has broken* HENRY's *near-trance. He leaps up.*)

HENRY (*Embracing him.*)
John!

JOHN
Welcome home. How's your overstuffed brain?

HENRY
I've forgotten everything already.

JOHN
At least you've got a diploma!

HENRY
No, I don't.

JOHN
Why not?

HENRY
They charge you a dollar. And I wouldn't pay it.

JOHN
But think how Mama would love it—your diploma from Harvard, framed on the wall!

HENRY
Let every sheep keep his own skin.

(JOHN *gives him a disparaging shove on the shoulder, and they tussle like boys. Breathless, they sit side by side.*)

John, I got more from one man—not even a professor—than I learned in four years of academic droning and snorting at Cambridge. And the strangest thing—he wasn't a stranger. I knew him, I'd seen him. You

7

know him. You walk by him on the street, you say hello; he's just a man, just a neighbor. *But* this man speaks and a hush falls over all of Harvard. And there's a light about him—that comes out of his face. But it's not the light of *one* man. I swear to you, John, it's the light of all Mankind!

JOHN (*Askance.*)

Idolator!

(HENRY *slaps the ground with the palm of his hand.*)

HENRY

Is this the Earth?

JOHN

I hope so.

HENRY (*Coming slowly to his feet.*)

No. It's you. And I. And God. And Mr. Emerson. And the Universal Mind!

JOHN

And Aunt Louisa?

HENRY

Yes, Aunt Louisa, too—false teeth and all.

(*Scratching his head.*)

It isn't easy to think of Aunt Louisa, swimming in the Milky Way. But that's the way of things, I'm sure of it.

JOHN

And if she can't keep afloat, you can dive in and save her!

(*They laugh.* JOHN *gets up, speaks more seriously.*)

Now that you've turned your backside on Harvard, what do you plan to do?

HENRY (*Pacing about.*)

Well, I think I'll *think* for a while. That'll be a change from college!

JOHN

But what do you want to *be*? Do you have any idea?

HENRY

Yes, I know exactly. I want to be as much as possible like Ralph Waldo Emerson.

(*The two brothers look at each other gravely. Light falls away from them. The light rises on* WALDO *and* LYDIAN. *He has the stature of a*

8

younger man, but he seems confused as he leafs through a manuscript.)

LYDIAN

Your lecture was splendid, dear.

WALDO

I think I read one paragraph twice. I lost my place.

LYDIAN

Nobody noticed, dear.

WALDO

If nobody noticed, then nobody was listening!

LYDIAN

They thought you did it for emphasis.

(WALDO *looks at his wife uncertainly. There is snoring from the other cell-cot.* HENRY, *during the* WALDO-LYDIAN *action, has returned to his own cot in the cell.*)

WALDO

(*Starts off, then turns to his wife again.*)
Did you see that one fellow? In the third row? With his eyes' closed. You don't think he was sleeping, do you?

LYDIAN

Concentrating, dear.

(*Almost reassured,* WALDO *moves off with his wife. The snoring grows to a crescendo as the key of moonlight rises in the prison cell.* HENRY *rises to a sitting position on his cot, looks at his sleeping cell-partner.*)

HENRY (*Gently.*)

My friend——
(*His fellow prisoner snorts, comes groggily awake.*)

OTHER COT

Huh? Why——?

HENRY

Every human being has an inalienable right to snore. *Provided* it does not interfere with the inalienable right of *other* men to snore.
(*The man on the other cot stares at him.*)
I couldn't hear what's going on.

OTHER COT

Nothin' goes on in here. Night half the time. Then day. Then night again. Don't make much difference.

9

HENRY

Sshh!

(HENRY *hears with every pore. There is the distant sound of a night-bird.*)

Did you hear that?

(*He comes to the imaginary downstage window.*)

OTHER COT (BAILEY)

I didn't hear nothin'. Just a bird.

HENRY (*Indignantly.*)

"Just a bird"! Can *you* make a cry like that? Or feed on flowers? Or carry the sky on your wings? Friend, you and I can't even fly.

(*There is a pause.* BAILEY *rubs his eyes.*)

BAILEY (*Foggily.*)

I missed part of that. Guess I'm not full awake.

HENRY (*Studying him.*)

Nobody is. If I ever met a man who was completely awake, how could I look him in the face?

BAILEY

What you do to get yourself locked up?

HENRY

What do you think?

BAILEY

Well-l-l—a man who talks educated like you—he can't 'a' done something small. Must be murder or worse.

HENRY

That's what I've done, by their lights, out there in the dark: murder or worse.

(*Change.*)

No. I refuse to commit murder. That's why I'm here.

BAILEY

Who they want you to kill?

HENRY

Mexico.

BAILEY

Who's that?

10

HENRY

That's where the war is.

BAILEY

What war?

HENRY (*Amazed, pacing.*)

Friend, this cell may be the only place in the United States that's at peace.

BAILEY

Who's fighting who?

HENRY

I'm not fighting anybody.

BAILEY

Neither'm I.

HENRY

But we've got a President who went out and boomed up a war all by himself—with no help from Congress and less help from me.

BAILEY

First I heered of it.

(*Warily.*)

Which side you on?

(*Pointing emphatically downstage, toward Concord.*)

Are you agin' *them*?

HENRY

"Them" . . . ?

BAILEY

Or are you *one* of them?

HENRY (*Thinks.*)

I'm one of Me.

BAILEY

That don't make no sense.

(*Far off, there is another bird-cry, forlornly wise. Again* HENRY *comes to the downstage imagined window.*)

HENRY

Hear that? Old friend of mine. He's a night flyer. Doesn't have to see where he's going—or maybe he can see what we can't. Or hear . . .

(*The bird cries again.* BAILEY *looks at* HENRY *as if he were a bit daft.*)
He's headed for the pond. Did you ever make friends with a loon?
(*There is a pause.*)

BAILEY

Not till tonight.

HENRY

Any time you hear a man called "loony," just remember that's a great compliment to the man and a great disrespect to the loon. A loon doesn't wage war, his government is perfect, being nonexistent. He is the world's best fisherman and completely in control of his senses, thank you.

(BAILEY *still is not sure about his new cellmate.*)
What are you here for, friend?

BAILEY

I'm waitin' trial.

HENRY

What did you do?

BAILEY

Nothin'.

HENRY

What do they *say* you did?

BAILEY (*Grudgingly.*)

Burned down a barn.
(*Defiantly.*)
But I didn't do it. All I did was snuck in to get some sleep and I guess the sparks from my pipe fell in the hay and——

HENRY

Tell 'em that!

BAILEY

The tellin' time is the trial. That's what I've been waitin' here for for three months.

HENRY (*Rising in a fury.*)

You've been locked up here for three entire months, waiting for a chance to say you're innocent?

BAILEY

That's about it.

HENRY
It's outrageous!
(*Calling.*)
Staples! Sam Staples!
(BAILEY *stops him.*)
BAILEY
Now don't make a ruckus. I'm not a troublemaker. I just want to earn
my keep, make a little tobakky money, and get along.
HENRY
"Get along"! Those words turn my stomach. Mister—what's your name?
BAILEY
Bailey.
(*A figure crosses the Village Square pompously.* HENRY *hears with
animal keenness.*)
HENRY
Mr. Bailey, listen! What do you hear?
BAILEY
Nothing—'cept footsteps.
HENRY
Footsteps of what?
BAILEY
A man, I guess.
HENRY
Where's he walking?
BAILEY
How would I know?
HENRY
I know where he's going. He's going where he's *supposed* to go. So he
can *be* where he's supposed to be, at the time he's supposed to be there.
Why? So he'll be *liked.* My God, a whole country of us who only want
to be liked.
(*Jutting his face squarely at* BAILEY.)
But to be *liked,* you must never disagree. And if you never disagree, it's
like only breathing *in* and never breathing *out!* A man can suffocate on
courtesy.
(*He paces.*)

What if God wanted to be *liked* instead of loved? What if the Almighty delayed every decision until He was sure it would please the majority? Great whales might have offended some legislature, which God knew would rise up some day to speak endlessly of the Common Good!

(*Vehemently.*)

Common Good be damned! Give me something magnificently *un*common!

BAILEY

I don't understand what you're sayin', but it's a marvel to hear the way the words roll out!

HENRY

I'll put it in plain Anglo-Saxon, Mr. Bailey: you're an uncommon man. You were protesting against the barn-builder who shut you in with clapboard and daily working hours.

BAILEY

Don't say that to no judge! If I burned down a barn, they'd throw me in jail.

HENRY

Friend, where do you think you are? You might as well have done the deed you didn't do!

BAILEY

But I'm not a man who goes around burning things down!

HENRY (*Thoughtfully.*)

Good for you. Fire *in*side burns hotter than fire *out*side. A man's conviction is stronger than a flame or a bullet or a rock.

(*Sinking onto the cot, thoughtfully.*)

I wonder if they'll keep *me* here three months, waiting trial! Who'll weed my bean patch?

(*A little laugh.*)

Of course, I might get some brain work done.

BAILEY

It feels good to talk to a smart fella. I bet you can even write.

HENRY

Sometimes.

14

BAILEY

I wish I was a writer. If I could write my name, I'd die happy.

HENRY

Then you'd do better than most writers. *Bailey's* not a hard name.

BAILEY

I know the start of it. It's the start of the alphabet backwards.

HENRY (*Stooping to the floor.*)

I'll teach you the rest!

(*A light comes up briefly on* HENRY's MOTHER.)

MOTHER

Oh, David Henry's an expert at getting things backward!

(*The light on her falls away.* HENRY *writes with his finger on the dust of the floor.* BAILEY *eagerly kneels beside him.*)

HENRY

B . . . A . . .

BAILEY

That's as far as I know.

HENRY

Who's Bailey?

BAILEY

I am.

HENRY

That's your next letter. I! I am I.

BAILEY

How do you write it?

HENRY (*Making a stroke in the dust.*)

Simple as a beanpole. Straight up and down. "B-A-I"—there, you're halfway through your name already. So you *turn the corner*—like this:

(*He draws an "L."*)

That's an "L"—B-A-I-"turn the corner." Now. Here's a rough one.

(*He squints up at the goggle-eyed* BAILEY.)

How much hair have you got?

BAILEY

Enough to comb.

HENRY

That's it. Bailey needs a comb to comb his hair!

(*Drawing in the dust.*)

There it is: "E"! And when you're all through, you want a nice tree to sit under. So you make a beanpole with branches on the top: that's "Y"!

(*He draws it.*)

And there's your name.

BAILEY

Jehosophat! You make it simple!

(*As he traces the letters on the dirt floor, turning to* HENRY *for approval.*)

"B-A-Beanpole-Turn the Corner-Comb-Tree."

HENRY

You've got it! Now you can write your name! "Bailey"!

BAILEY

I'll leave this jail an educated man!

(*Abruptly.*)

You must be a teacher!

HENRY

Being a teacher is like being in jail: once it's on your record, you can never get rid of it.

(HENRY *takes the chair from the cell and places it at the foremost edge of the thrust.* BAILEY *sinks into shadows on his cot, rehearsing his name from the letters on the floor.*

HENRY *becomes the young schoolmaster, addressing the audience as if they were a classroom full of unseen children.*)

Students, hold your hand up in front of you, like this.

(*He looks about to see that they are all doing just as he is: holding the open palm of the hand eighteen inches in front of the face.*)

Is there anything between my nose and my fingers? Nothing? My young friends, there are millions of tiny, dancing particles, whizzing back and forth, running into each other, and bouncing off! Stars, worlds, planets, universes. Right here!

(*He blows a puff of breath into the empty space, then claps his hands together.* BALL, *a pompous townsman with a silver-topped cane, stalks in, listening to the end of* HENRY's *remarks to the schoolroom.*)

And now—I give you a mystery! How do we *know* that these particles are there?

(HENRY *flicks his other hand through the seeming emptiness in front of him.*)

BALL

How indeed?

(HENRY *is startled, turns, sees the pompous visitor—then addresses the class.*)

HENRY

Ah, we have a surprise guest in the classroom today. The Chairman of the Concord School Committee, Deacon Nehemiah Ball.

BALL

I am not here to interrupt your scheduled curriculum.

(*He pronounces it English-style: "sheduled."*)

HENRY

Thank you, sir. These particles——

BALL

Just an observer, that's all I am.

(HENRY *is getting irritated.* BALL *folds his arms behind his back, his cane dangles tail-like behind him;* HENRY *starts to speak again, but* BALL *interrupts.*)

HENRY

Scientists have——

BALL

Try to forget I'm in the room.

HENRY (*Clearing his throat.*)

We'll try, sir.

(*To his class.*)

Now. In recent years, scientists have discovered that——

BALL

How is it that I see no school books open here?

HENRY

We're . . . huckleberrying, sir.

BALL

You're what?

HENRY

We're scrambling for ideas the way we hunt for huckleberries in the woods.

BALL

That's no way to learn anything. All they need to know is clearly spelled out in the approved school texts.

HENRY

All, Deacon Ball? Young Potter, here—

(*Pointing to a student in the first row.*)

—just asked me if I really think there is a God.

BALL

Young heathen!

HENRY

He simply asked why, since we never *see* God, should we believe He exists?

BALL (*Addressing Potter.*)

Matters of Theology, boy, are discussable with your spiritual leader.

HENRY

Potter has already asked his "spiritual leader"—but the Reverend Whoever-It-Is called him an atheist! For committing the primary sin of *doubt*.

(*To the student.*)

Mr. Potter, I'll try to answer you just as I once replied to the same question put to me by an annoying, inquisitive young man—myself.

BALL (*Narrowly.*)

Will this be a *theological* opinion?

HENRY (*Slowly.*)

It will be a *human* opinion.

(*Again to the student, reasonably.*)

If I go into a shop and see all the nicely finished wheels, gears, pinions, springs of a *watch* lying spread out on a bench, then later find them put together exactly and working in unison to move the hands across a dial and show the passage of time, do I believe that these pieces have been flung together by blind chance? Certainly not. I believe that somebody with *thought* and plan and power has been there. An IN-TELLIGENCE!

(WALDO, *in academic robes, has come to a pulpit in his area.*)

WALDO

An Intelligence governs the universe. And in this worship service we shall celebrate our gratitude to that Intelligence. Let us pray.

(*He lowers his head, praying silently.*)

HENRY

Nor do I think that the sun rising above Concord this morning was an accident. I hope you saw it, Mr. Potter. And you, too, Deacon Ball. It was a brilliant sunrise.

(*Emphatically.*)

We are all related, Mr. Potter—and interrelated to a *Universal Mind.*

BALL

That's atheism!

(*It is not easy for* HENRY *to restrain himself.*)

HENRY

I've often wondered, Deacon Ball, if atheism might even be popular with God himself.

BALL (*Shocked.*)

Transcendental blasphemy!

WALDO

The Universal Mind is the divine part of all of us; and we partake, knowingly or not, in the wonder of that Universal Mind.

(*The light falls away on* WALDO, *but he remains at the pulpit in meditation.*)

HENRY (*Softly.*)

Does all this make any sense to you, Potter?

BALL

It makes no sense to me. You will teach the textbooks, sir!

HENRY

I find your texts somewhat behind the century.

BALL

You find them so!

HENRY

Yes, sir, I do!

BALL

And you choose to ignore the books which have been *pro*scribed by the School Committee?

HENRY

My students have the ache of curiosity, which I'm afraid your *pro*scriptions will not cure!

(*There are a couple of young laughs—quickly stifled. They seem to come from the class.* BALL *turns stern eyes toward the imagined pupils.*)

BALL (*Imperiously.*)

Silence! You will show respect for your elders! And you, Schoolmaster, will teach strictly according to text! No *huckleberrying!*

HENRY (*After a pause.*)

Class. You've heard the Deacon. We shall stick to the approved books. Your eyes must not wander from the page—to look at a leaf, or an unauthorized butterfly. You must not listen to a cricket or smell a flower that has not been approved by the School Committee. You'd better close both ears and hold your nose—though you may have to grow an extra hand to do it.

(*He pantomimes the difficulty of covering successively two ears, then his nose and one ear, then the other ear and his nose. At this there is uninhibited laughter from the unseen classroom—through a loudspeaker at the foot of the thrust.*)

BALL (*Waddling to the forestage.*)

Silence! Is this the gratitude you show to the municipality which feeds your minds?

(*The veins bulge in his forehead, he pounds with his silver-topped cane.*)

You will show decent respect!

(*The laughter continues.* BALL *turns to* HENRY.)

Make them be silent, sir!

(HENRY *simply lifts his hand; the laughter stops.*)

The lack of order in this classroom will most certainly be reported to the full School Committee, which I intend to call into extraordinary session tonight.

(JOHN *appears, speaks as if to* HENRY's *mind.*)

20

JOHN

Henry, give the man a penny apology. Two-cents-worth of humility!

HENRY

Why should I?

JOHN

So they won't cut you off from the class. If you're stubborn, what will happen when Potter asks questions?

(*A pause—then* HENRY *makes the supreme effort at contrition. He takes a deep breath, turns to face* BALL.)

HENRY (*With much difficulty.*)

Deacon Ball. I'm sorry that you've had a rather ragged time in my classroom today. I have intended no offense to you or the School Committee.

BALL

Well, we've come to expect a certain degree of unruliness from Harvard men. Your apology shows that you recognize this flaw in your character. But your students don't have Harvard as an excuse. They must be punished.

HENRY

I shall lecture them.

BALL

You will *flog* them!

HENRY (*Stunned.*)

What?

BALL

You will flog them—for showing irreverence to authority!

HENRY (*Defiantly.*)

No, sir!

BALL

I beg your pardon.

HENRY

I said "No." I do not believe in corporal punishment.

BALL

What you believe is irrelevant. Your opinion, as a teacher, has not been asked for. I direct you to FLOG!

(HENRY *hesitates.*)

HENRY

Why?

BALL

It is policy. Offending students are whipped.

HENRY

And what would that teach them?

BALL

Obedience. An essential quality in subordinates, whether they are pupils in a classroom or soldiers on a battlefield.

HENRY

They are not training to be soldiers. Not *my* students.

BALL

These young people are not *yours.* They have been sent to you by the tax-paying citizens of Concord, who expect you to abide by the rules laid down by the school administrators.

(*Silence.* HENRY *does not move.*)

Perform your duty, Schoolmaster Thoreau, if you expect to retain your post in this community.

(HENRY *slowly unbuckles his belt, then whips it off, taking a short step toward* BALL, *who pulls back, thinking perhaps* HENRY *is about to flog him. Then* HENRY *turns front, to the class.*)

HENRY (*Bitterly, to his class.*)

Six of you. *Any* six. Come forward. It doesn't matter who. You are all —*all* of you—accused of the damning crimes of laughter, curiosity, and candid self-expression! Bigelow!

(HENRY *grabs the chair, spins it over as if he were putting a boy across his knee. Eyes closed,* HENRY *lashes the chair fiercely and painfully with his belt.*)

Coleman!

(*Again he lashes the chair.*)

Loring!

(*Another lash.*)

McClain!

(*He whips the chair again, blindly, loathing what he is doing.*)

Henderson.

(*Another lash. Then a hesitation.*)

22

Potter!

(*This whipping is the most painful of all. He turns his head away. Now finished, breathless,* HENRY *opens his eyes, stares at the belt as if it were something filthy and revolting. He flings it away from him, far offstage.*)

BALL

I congratulate you. I am happy to be able to report to the School Committee that Schoolmaster Thoreau——

HENRY

—has administered the Sacrament of the Schoolroom; and he resigns as a "teacher" in the Public Schools of Concord!

(BALL *icily falls back into the shadows and disappears. The light on the pulpit comes up in full brilliance on* WALDO.)

WALDO (*In the midst of an inner struggle.*)

—but I cannot comply with custom! I cannot perform the rites required of me by this congregation. For I have searched the Scriptures and can find nothing which calls on us to repeat endlessly the ceremony of the Last Supper. Intellectually, emotionally, spiritually, I cannot administer this Sacrament. So I resign my position as pastor of the Second Unitarian Church of Boston.

(HENRY *has put the chair—his "student"—back in the jail cell. Sadly he comes down into the light.*)

HENRY

I shall never teach again.

WALDO

I shall never preach again.

(*Light rises on* MOTHER *and* JOHN.)

MOTHER

Have you ever noticed, John, how much Mr. Emerson talks like our David Henry?

(JOHN *notices the disconsolate* HENRY *and goes to him.*)

JOHN (*Quietly.*)

A school doesn't need a School Committee. Or Trustees. Or Governors. Or Lumber. Or approved textbooks. All a school needs is a mind that sends, and minds that receive.

23

HENRY

Nobody can teach anybody anything.

JOHN (*Blithely.*)

Of course not. Teach them how to teach themselves.

HENRY (*Fired with an idea.*)

Our *own* school, John. No buildings. Break out of the classroom prison. All we need is *sky!*

(*The cyclorama becomes ablaze with blue, and sunlit clouds. There is the screech and wheeling of birds, and a great sense of freedom.*)

The *universe* can be our schoolroom, John—the great, vast world of the Concord countryside.

(HENRY *claps a broad straw hat on his head, sticks a notebook under his arm. There is a flood of light on the forestage.* HENRY *seems to be marching across the open sunlit fields.* JOHN *follows with a telescope.*)

Students!

(*The* STUDENTS, *though imaginary, are presumably all around him.*)

Watch! Notice! Observe!

(*He takes the telescope from* JOHN *and uses it as a pointer.*)

See what is happening around you. Did you ever have any· idea so much was going on in Heywood's Meadow? I'll wager even Heywood doesn't know.

(*A discovery.*)

The cypripedium is already in flower!

(*He leafs back through his notebook.*)

Last year it didn't bloom until tomorrow!

(*He makes an entry in his notebook.*)

Do you know how few people know what we've just discovered? Stumbling on the first morning of a new flower! Most of Concord is too busy eating meals and going to the postoffice!

(*A strikingly beautiful girl—twenty perhaps—stands at the edge of the light, watching and listening, fascinated.*)

Oh, I would be sad and sorry to remember that I once was in the world and noticed nothing remarkable. Not so much as a prince in disguise.

(*Looking sideways at his brother.*)

John, are you a prince in disguise?

JOHN
Of course.

(HENRY *paces about the meadow.*)

HENRY
Wouldn't it be dreadful if I had lived in the Golden Age as a *hired man?* Or visited Olympus, and fell asleep after dinner—and completely missed the conversation of the gods. Or imagine living in Judea eighteen hundred years ago—and never knowing that Jesus was my contemporary! What are you doing?

(*He has, in his peripatetic outpouring, come face-to-face with the girl, who has taken out a notebook; she is absorbed in writing, jarred by his question.*)

ELLEN
I'm writing.

HENRY
What?

ELLEN
What you've been saying. So I'll remember.

HENRY
Don't just remember what I said. Remember what I'm talking about. (*Obediently, she closes her notebook.* HENRY *crosses to* JOHN, *lowering his voice.*)
Who's that?

JOHN
It's a girl.

(*Both stare at her, impressed.*)

HENRY
One of ours? I mean, does she belong to us? Is she one of our students?

JOHN (*Taking a good look at her.*)
I wouldn't mind. Would you?

HENRY (*Crossing back to her.*)
Excuse me, Miss. But I think you're a little old to be a member of this class.

JOHN
Henry, a young lady is never too old for anything.

HENRY

It's just that—well—most of our students are twelve—or thereabouts. And you're—well, not exactly thereabouts.

(*The girl laughs.*)

ELLEN

Does it make so much difference really? I just want to come along and listen and watch. I won't be any bother or ask any questions.

HENRY

Why not?

ELLEN

My little brother is the only one who has the right to ask questions: he's paying tuition.

HENRY

(*Points a finger at her.*)

You're Sewell.

JOHN

How'd you know?

HENRY

If I can spot a cypripedium, I can spot a Sewell.

JOHN

There's only one rule in this class: no rules. So, of course, you're welcome to come along—any time you like.

ELLEN

What about tuition?

JOHN

You've already paid it. If you were ugly, we'd charge you. Or twelve. Or thereabouts.

(ELLEN *and* JOHN *laugh.* HENRY *does not; he merely looks at her.*)

ELLEN

You're John Thoreau.

(*Turning.*)

And you're the thundercloud. Henry.

(HENRY *frowns.*)

HENRY

What previous educational experience have you had?

ELLEN
Finishing school.

HENRY
Dear God.

ELLEN
I survived.

HENRY
I warn you, Miss Sewell, that John and I are not finishers. Nobody leaves us with a smooth surface. We rough up the consciousness, scrape the moss off young minds.

ELLEN
Please, Mr. Thoreau. Go back to your students. I've interrupted.

HENRY
Of course you have. Every creative event that ever happened in the world was an interruption. Unexpected. Unplanned for. The only people who ever get anyplace interesting are the people who get lost. That's why the planets are so much better company than the stars—they keep wandering back and forth across the sky and you never know where you're going to find them.
(*To the unseen class.*)
Students. We have another Sewell. Edmund's sister.
(*To the girl.*)
You have a first name?

ELLEN
Ellen.

HENRY
Ellen Sewell. Our textbook, Miss Sewell, is Heywood's Meadow. Approved by the Almighty, if not by the School Committee.
(*To the class.*)
In this single pasture, there are *three hundred* distinct and separate varieties of grass. I know; I have catalogued them myself. You look down and you say: "That's grass. Grass is grass." Ridiculous. You have missed the splendid variety of the show. There's camel grass, candy grass, cloud grass, cow-quake, mouse-barley, fox-tail, London-lace, devil's knitting needle, feather-top, buffalo grass, timothy and

barnyard grass and clovers enough to sweeten the bellies of all the lambs since creation.

(ELLEN *has taken down her notebook and is writing. Suddenly* HENRY *leans down, seeing something, and plucks an imaginary blade of grass.*) John, look at this. What would you say it is?

HENRY

It's *Coix Lacryma-jobi,* which means Job's Tears. I've never seen a specimen here. Students, I beg your pardon. We are in the midst of three hundred and *one* varieties of God-made grasses.

JOHN

I've never seen it before.

HENRY

It's *Coix Lacryma-jobi,* which means Job's Tears. I've never seen a specimen here. Students, I beg your pardon. We are in the midst of three hundred and *one* varieties of God-made grasses.

(*He jots this information in his notebook. Out of the corner of his eye, he sees* ELLEN *writing.*) You're writing again.

ELLEN

Just "Job's Tears."

HENRY

Why?

ELLEN

When you go to school, you're supposed to write things down, so you remember what you've been taught.

HENRY

Then it's the notebook that does the remembering, not you.

ELLEN

You keep a notebook.

HENRY

I also wear a ridiculous straw hat. That doesn't mean that *you* should wear a ridiculous hat. You'd look ridiculous in it. Nature didn't stuff this meadow full of identical blades of grass, each an imitation of another. They're all *different!* Follow-the-leader is not the game we're playing here! Young lady, BE YOUR OWN MAN!

JOHN (*Low.*)

Henry, don't shout at her.

ELLEN

I won't take notes. I promise you. Not one.

HENRY

Why not? If you want to take notes, go ahead. But not because I'm doing it, or because I told you to.

(*Gently.*)

Miss Sewell, I want you to be yourself—not your idea of what you think is somebody else's idea of yourself.

(*Turning to the students.*)

Perhaps, students, Miss Sewell's interruption has given us the essence of the textbook we call Heywood's Meadow. The multiple grasses beneath our feet. The infinity of the sky above us.

(*Riffling through his notebook.*)

And if I have jotted down a note about a cloud-flame, or about sunlight on bird-wings, don't you write, just because *I* am writing. Don't ape me, or copy me.

(*Intensely, but quietly.*)

If you wish merely to *listen* to the sky, or *smell* the sky, or *feel* the sky with your finger-tips, do that, too!

(*With great conviction.*)

Because I think there should be as many different persons in the world as possible. So—*each of you*—be very careful to find out and pursue your own way!

(*As the lights dim on the sunlit field,* HENRY *goes back to the dimly-lit cell.*)

BAILEY (*Rapturously.*)

Bailey, Bailey, Bailey! I kin write! Watch! Watch me do it all by myself—!

(BAILEY *starts again to trace his name in the dust on the cell floor.* HENRY *bitterly erases the pattern of letters in the dust with his foot.* BAILEY *looks up, puzzled.*)

HENRY

Don't learn to write your name.

BAILEY

I already learned.

HENRY (*Splenetic.*)

Unlearn it. Writing your name can lead to writing sentences. And the next thing you'll be doing is writing paragraphs, and then books. And then you'll be in as much trouble as I am!

BAILEY (*Wonderingly.*)

You write books?

(HENRY *sits on the cot.*)

HENRY (*Wryly.*)

Yes.

BAILEY

If my mother'd lived to see me sittin' in the same jail cell with a man who writ a book, ohhhh-ee, she'd be proud of me. Tell me somethin'. Do you make up all the words yourself?

HENRY

Oh, now and then I stick in a word or two that's been used before. The base trick is to pick the right words and put 'em in the right order.

BAILEY

Must be a fortune in it. I hear tell some books cost more'n a dollar!

HENRY

But they haven't been perfected yet. They've gotta put legs on them. As it is now, a book just sits in a shop and has to wait for somebody with legs on to come in and find it.

BAILEY (*Blankly.*)

Oh?

(BAILEY *has taken tobacco from his rough coat in the locker, thus freeing the box for the next scene.*)

HENRY

My first book—also my last book—was a very stationary model. The publisher brought out a thousand copies!—and gave me the privilege of paying for the printing. So all the copies that didn't sell belonged to the author. And they came running home to me, legs or not.

(*Gravely.*)

Right now, Mr. Bailey, I have a library of nearly nine hundred volumes!—seven hundred of which I wrote myself.

(*Pointing to the scuffed-up letters in the dust of the floor.*)

My friend, give up your literary career.

(*Suddenly,* HENRY *takes the locker-box from the cell, flips it over, open-*

side up, and drags it down onto the thrust. JOHN *comes on, helping him with the "boat."*)

HENRY

John, today I thought we'd make a complete circuit of the pond. If this boat isn't large enough for the whole class, I'll take the first trip, you take the second.

JOHN

It'll be large enough.

HENRY

We lost another pupil?

JOHN

No. We lost two.

HENRY (*Defensively.*)

Good. Education should not be a mass process!

JOHN

With us, it isn't.

HENRY

The whole idea of our school is that the size of the classroom grows larger and larger—

JOHN

—while the size of the class grows smaller and smaller.

HENRY

How many do we actually have left?

JOHN (*Avoiding his eyes.*)

Mother's got the name of a new family, just moved to Concord.

HENRY

How many children?

JOHN

Be patient, Henry. The wife is pregnant.

(JOHN *starts to leave.*)

HENRY

Where are you going?

JOHN

Back to the pencil factory.

HENRY

Why?

JOHN

It might be a little overpowering—to have twice as many teachers as pupils.

HENRY

Only one left?

(JOHN *goes off.* HENRY, *alone, scowls, kicks at the box-boat.* ELLEN *appears.*)

ELLEN

Mr. Thoreau—?

(HENRY *turns.*)

HENRY

Good morning——

ELLEN

I—I came to tell you that you shouldn't wait for Edmund. Just go ahead and start the class without him. He—uh—won't be coming today.

HENRY

I hope he's not ill?

ELLEN

No.

(*Pause.*)

It's my Father——

HENRY

He's ill?

ELLEN

Not exactly. Father's worried—because he thinks Edmund's learning too much.

HENRY

That's good news. I thought Edmund was a bit sluggish myself. Compared with the other students. That is, when we had other students to compare him with.

(*Briskly.*)

Well, tell your Father not to worry. I'll slow down with Edmund.

ELLEN

I'm afraid Father doesn't want him to come to your school at all any more.

HENRY (*Bridling.*)

Oh. Your Father's opposed to knowledge.

ELLEN

No. He's opposed to Transcendentalists. That's what he says you are. And your brother, too. "A whole family afflicted with Transcendentalism."

HENRY

What the devil does your Father think Transcendentalism *is?*

ELLEN

I asked him and he tried to explain it to me. And the more he explained, the less I understood it. Father has a gift that way.

HENRY

A born *non*-teacher.

(*Suddenly.*)

Miss Sewell. Get into the boat.

ELLEN

Oh?

HENRY

Since I find myself unexpectedly unemployed, I shall take you on a voyage of exploration. No tuition charge.

(HENRY *helps her into the boat.*)

Keep your eye on the line between the water and the sky. I'll row.

(*He pantomimes pushing the boat off; the light narrows, the background trembles with the wavering pattern of sunlight reflected from water. With no visible oars, he rows. Suddenly, he points.*)

There used to be a row of cedars on that far shore.

(*Sighing.*)

But we have lost that link with Lebanon.

ELLEN

Where have they gone?

HENRY

Into firewood—and up in smoke. Into houses. Do you know what we're doing, Miss Sewell? We're poisoning paradise. Shearing off the woods, making the poor earth bald before her time.

ELLEN

But we have to have houses, Mr. Thoreau. Or should we all live in caves?

HENRY

What's the use of a house if you haven't got a tolerable planet to put it on? Did you know that trees cry out in pain when they're cut? I've heard them. But what bells in town toll for them? We prosecute men for abusing children; we ought to prosecute them for maltreating nature.

ELLEN

My father says God put everything here for men to *use*.

HENRY

Oh? Did the Good Father put us here to root and snort and glut ourselves like pigs? No, the pigs are better; pigs may be the most respectable part of the population: at least they consume the rubble instead of contributing to it.

(*In the distance, the whistle of a railroad train.*)

Hear that? There goes a carload of two-legged pigs, off to market . . . emasculating the landscape with their tracks . . .

ELLEN

I rather like the railroad. Far better than a horse and carriage.

HENRY

Why?

ELLEN

It's smoother, and much faster.

HENRY

And dirtier. And uglier. Thank God men haven't learned to fly: they'd lay waste the sky as well as the earth . . . chop down the clouds!

ELLEN (*Somewhat puzzled.*)

Is that in Transcendentalism, Mr. Thoreau?

HENRY (*Laughs.*)

No. Yes, it is—in a way. Take your father. Do you love the man?

ELLEN

Of course.

HENRY

Why?

ELLEN

He's my father.

34

HENRY

Is he beautiful?

ELLEN

Dear me, no!

HENRY

Does he create beauty? Paint? Play a musical instrument?

ELLEN

No.

HENRY (*Pointing up, then down.*)

Can he fly like that bird? Or swim, like that fellow down there?

ELLEN

He can swim a little. He used to. But not like that fish.

HENRY

Nevertheless you *love* him.

ELLEN

Of course.

HENRY

Your love *transcends* what your father is—and what he is not. Every consciousness is capable of going beyond itself. Every——

(ELLEN *frowns a bit.*)

Dammit, I've lost you. Put your hand in the water.

(*She does.*)

Can you touch bottom?

ELLEN (*Reaching down.*)

It's too deep.

HENRY

For the length of your arm. Not for the length of your mind.

(*He has stopped rowing.*)

Miss Sewell. Why should your reach stop with your skin? When you transcend the limits of yourself, you can cease merely living—and begin to BE!

ELLEN

I don't mind *living*——

HENRY

But *being* is so much more interesting.

ELLEN (*Taking her hand out of the "water."*)
I'm a little bit afraid—just—to "be"!

HENRY
Think how free it is. If you're never afraid.

ELLEN
Aren't you ever afraid?
(*He thinks, stares at her.*)

HENRY
Yes. I'm afraid that I might "live" right through this moment—and *only* live—
(*He leans forward on his oars, looking into her face.*)
—look at you and only *see* you. Oh, it doesn't hurt at all to look at you, believe me. But what if there's more—and I miss it?

ELLEN
Miss what?

HENRY
What if all that is beautiful, in women, in the world—or worlds—what if all of it is totaled up in this face here, in front of me—and I am empty enough to think I am merely seeing *one* face?
(ELLEN *doesn't follow him precisely, but she's pleased.*)

ELLEN
That's Transcendentalism?
(HENRY *has lost interest in Transcendentalism and is more interested in* ELLEN.)

HENRY (*Resumes rowing.*)
If you like.

ELLEN
I don't think that's wicked. I think it's rather nice.

HENRY
Who says it's wicked?

ELLEN
Father. Last night at the dinner table, Edmund gave Father a sermon on the Over-Soul.

HENRY
Good for Edmund! Most dining rooms are tabernacles where only the father gets the pulpit.

36

ELLEN

Oh, Father got it right back. He was still shouting at breakfast. He broke off with an incomplete sentence last night, and picked it right up this morning at porridge.

HENRY

Well, I'm a little older than Edmund. But I have yet to hear the first syllable of valuable advice from my seniors.

(*His eyes going to the horizon.*)

We are born as innocents. We are polluted by advice. Here is life in front of us, like the surface of this pond, inviting us to sail on it. A voyage, an experiment. Waiting to be performed. Has your father tried it before? That's no help to me. Or to you. Keep your innocence, Edmund!

ELLEN

Ellen.

HENRY

Ellen, yes. You look very much alike, you know. The eyes. You both listen with your eyes.

ELLEN

I have to go back.

HENRY

Why?

ELLEN

Father expects me.

HENRY

Surprise him.

ELLEN

Edmund did. He's braver than I am.

HENRY

Stand up to your father!

(*He stands. The boat rocks.*)

ELLEN

Please, Mr. Thoreau—not in the boat!

HENRY

Oh——

(*He sits.*)

ELLEN

Will you row me back to shore, please?

HENRY

No. Listen to me. If I were to say, "I Love You, Sewell—Miss Sewell. Ellen"—you wouldn't think much of it as a statement of fact if you knew it was just an echo, a mouthing, of something somebody *told* me to say.

(*Disparagingly.*)

Some *father!*

(*Quietly.*)

But if I say "I love you" out of myself, out of my own experience— or lack of it—out of my innocence, then you and God had better believe me.

(*The light comes up on* JOHN *and* MOTHER, *as* ELLEN *turns away from* HENRY, *staring at the water.*)

JOHN (*Running in.*)

Mother, Henry's in love.

MOTHER (*Worried.*)

Who's he in love with?

JOHN

A girl.

MOTHER

Thank God.

(*Light falls away on* JOHN *and* MOTHER.)

ELLEN (*Icily.*)

I'm not one of your fish, nor one of your birds, Mr. Thoreau. So I can neither swim nor fly back to dry land. I must simply sit here and hope that you are gentleman enough to row me ashore.

(HENRY *doesn't move. He looks at her. She's beautiful, but he knows he's missed his chance, and it frustrates him.*)

HENRY (*With a sigh.*)

Miss Sewell. I apologize. And I'll row you to shore on one condition.

ELLEN

I have to accept it.

HENRY

Come to church on Sunday.

ELLEN

You don't go to church.

HENRY

Of course not. I can't stand sitting in a pew, having the Sabbath despoiled by a sermon.

ELLEN

But still you invite me to church?

HENRY

With John. *We* have a strong family resemblance, too. And if you find a single syllable in me worth writing in a notebook, you'll find *paragraphs* of it in John! Where I am cantankerous, he is amiable. Where I am thorns and brambles, he is a garden. Where I am a bare hill in winter, he is spring.

(*He begins to row, slowly.*)

ELLEN

How do you know that your brother would want to take me to church?

HENRY

Didn't you notice that day in Heywood's Meadow—when he proposed to you?

ELLEN

He barely spoke to me.

HENRY

That's why you didn't hear him. You missed the eloquence of his silence.

(*The boat presumably comes to shore.* HENRY *jumps out, pantomimes pulling it onto the bank, then helps* ELLEN *as she steps out.* ELLEN, *having won her point, wonders . . . have I really lost?*)

ELLEN (*With mixed pride and regret.*)

Good day, Mr. Thoreau. Thank you for making Transcendentalism so clear.

HENRY

Did I? If there's anything I missed, just ask Edmund.

ELLEN

What will happen to your school?

HENRY (*Turning away.*)

I'm going back to it. As a pupil. Maybe I can learn from Nature—

and from John: a pasture can be raucous with flowers, and not make a single sound. But a man—presumably wiser than a daffodil—can beat so loudly on the eardrums that nobody hears what he's trying to say.

(ELLEN *is bewildered. Then, in his silence,* HENRY *seems almost fierce to her, and she runs off, frightened. He looks wistfully toward the air where* ELLEN *was. Then he stares down into the empty boat, kicks it. That emptiness is something of the vacancy he feels within himself.*

Slowly, HENRY *moves up into the area of the jail cell. The wavering pattern of light-on-water falls away. Only the long nocturnal shadows of the cell remain.* BAILEY *is asleep on his cot, snoring lightly.* HENRY *looks down at him.*)

HENRY

Mr. Bailey, what do you think of marriage?

(BAILEY *gives out a derisive snore, which suggests that subconsciously he may have heard the question.* HENRY *nods.*)

That seems to be the majority opinion.

(*He settles back on his own cot. The clock strikes eleven. The sound dilates, louder and louder, pulsing with standing waves.*)

Bailey, did you hear that? I don't think I've ever felt those waves of sound from the clock tower.

(*A laugh.*)

That's ridiculous—that a man has to be put in a stone box before he can hear the music of his own village!

(HENRY *calls through the barred window.*)

Thank you, Concord! Thank you for locking me up so I'm free to hear what I've never heard before. You put me behind iron bars and walls four feet thick! How do you know that *I'm* not the free one? The freest man in the world! And you, out there, are chained to what you have to do tomorrow morning!

(*Now he whispers through the cell grating.*)

Speak softly, Concord—I can hear you breathing.

(BAILEY *lets out a snore.*)

Quiet, Bailey. We free men should listen to the cry of prisoners.

(*The light falls away on the cell. There is the projection of a stained glass window.*

Facing upstage is a standing row of worshipers: DEACON BALL, SAM

STAPLES, WALDO, LYDIAN, MRS. THOREAU, JOHN *and* ELLEN *beside him, and townspeople. All are dressed Sunday-best and singing the last stanza of a hymn: "Blest Be the Tie that Binds," Pilgrim Hymnal 272.*)

CHURCHGOERS (*Singing in unison.*)

> Blest be the tie that binds
> Our hearts in Christian love;
> The Fellowship of kindred minds
> Is like to that Above.
> A-men.

(*Halfway through the hymn,* EDWARD *scratches his bottom.* LYDIAN *pulls his hand away.*

After the "Amen" there is the swell of organ music, as the worshipers begin to file out into the tree-dappled light of a Sunday noon. ELLEN *comes out, on* JOHN's *arm. There is a cluster of conversation around the* EMERSONS.)

DEACON BALL

Tell me, Doctor Emerson. What is the feeling of a clergyman when he hears another pastor in the pulpit?

WALDO

Relief.

DEACON

That you don't have to give the sermon?

WALDO (*Drily.*)

That it's over.

(*The* MOTHER *is beaming at* JOHN *and* ELLEN. *Suddenly she sees something which turns her soul to ice. The others look, with varying degrees of shock, as* HENRY, *his shirt unbuttoned, pushes a wheelbarrow full of earth. Blithely he crosses directly in front of the washed and starched churchgoers.* ELLEN *looks down,* JOHN *suppresses a grin,* WALDO *and* LYDIAN *turn gracefully away, and* DEACON BALL *tries to look as much as possible like Moses on the mountain.*)

MOTHER

Oh, David Henry! *Not* on Sunday!

HENRY (*Pleasantly.*)

This *is* Sunday, isn't it. Have all of you been shut up inside? On this beautiful morning? What a pity!

41

DEACON

We've been feeding our souls!

HENRY

How selfish of you.

(*He reaches into the wheelbarrow and sprinkles some of the unseen contents at the feet of the churchgoers.*)

I've been feeding the flora of Concord.

(*They wince at the aroma.*)

Bringing loaves and fishes to the lilacs.

(*Waving cheerfully,* HENRY *trundles the wheelbarrow off. All eyes follow him.*)

DEACON

Labor on the Sabbath, and the Devil's in Massachusetts.

JOHN

Henry worships in the woods.

DEACON BALL

Then what do we have churches for?

WALDO

I sometimes wonder.

LYDIAN (*Quickly.*)

Dr. Emerson means that the Good Lord is everywhere.

DEACON BALL

The Lord *I* know rested on the Seventh Day.

WALDO

Why, Deacon Ball, you're older than I thought!

(*Before* BALL *can really take offense, the warm-hearted* EMERSON *pats his shoulder.*)

For you and me, Deacon, the Declaration of Independence has already been written. Young Thoreau has to declare it every day—Sundays included.

(*Starting off, with* LYDIAN.)

So what's the harm if he sweats his psalms instead of singing them?

(*The worshipers disperse.* JOHN *and* ELLEN *go off together.* MRS. THOREAU *is left alone.* SHE *looks off toward the vanished* HENRY.)

MOTHER

Oh, David Henry—why did God and I have to make you so peculiar?

(*Eyes to heaven.*)

And please, dear Lord, don't let John get too strange. Perhaps, if it isn't too much trouble, you could slip the word "yes" into that young lady's mouth. Amen.

(She goes off. The stained glass window fades. The cyclorama becomes sunlit clouds. Amplified and echoing, JOHN's *laughter spills across the open field.* HENRY *comes on, takes a triumphant stance.)*

HENRY

She said "Yes!!!"

*(*JOHN *bursts on, almost drunk with his own laughter.)*

Congratulations—I'm happy for you, John! Are you going to do it right away? Or do you have to go through those tribal rites—posting the banns, all that primitive nonsense?

*(*JOHN, *in a paroxysm of laughter, embraces his brother.)*

JOHN

She said—she said——

(He breaks off again, laughing.)

HENRY

She said "Yes," naturally!

*(*JOHN, *laughing, can't answer.)*

She didn't say "No!"?

JOHN

No, she didn't say "No!"

HENRY

What the devil *did* she say?

JOHN *(Still laughing.)*

She quoted her father.

HENRY

Heavenly or here?

JOHN

The one her mother married.

HENRY

Well, what did old Porridge-Face have to say?

JOHN

He said——

(Laughing.)

She said he said . . . that marriage to either of the Thoreau brothers was unthinkable!

HENRY

Amen! The Thoreau brothers never had any intention of marrying her father!

(*Hopefully.*)

But she stood up to him?

JOHN

I wasn't there—but evidently she sat down.

(*He sits.*)

HENRY

So you wasted six good summer Sundays taking her to church!

JOHN

I swear to you, I didn't pray. I kept looking at that face out of the corner of my eye. Wondering what she was thinking. I finally realized she wasn't thinking at all!

HENRY

She's a girl. Who'd want a wife who went around thinking?

JOHN (*Starts laughing again.*)

When I asked her to marry me, there was a pregnant pause. Well, not pregnant, but a pause. Then she said: "Oh, dear . . ." At first, I thought she was being affectionate, then I realized she was only saying, "Oh, dear!"

HENRY

Then what?

JOHN

Then she said, "Why doesn't Henry ask me?" And I said, "If he does, will you say yes?" And she said, "No, but why doesn't he ask me anyhow?"

HENRY

It's an outrage! She wants to wear *both* of our scalps on her petticoat strings!

JOHN

She won't marry you, and she won't marry me. But I think she'd marry *us* in a minute.

HENRY

That's carrying Unitarianism too far!

JOHN

If we were Mohammedans——

44

HENRY

Wouldn't help. Moslems take multiple wives, not multiple husbands.

JOHN

But then, Henry, I destroyed the whole thing. I killed it. I laughed.
(HENRY *laughs a little.*)
Not like that. Bigger!
(*They both begin to laugh.*)
Not at her, the dear girl; at *us!* I almost shattered the most sacred
tradition of the Thoreau tribe: celibacy!

HENRY (*Laughing.*)

You're a good-hearted man, John! You saved the girl from marrying a
monk.

JOHN

Or a pair of them!
(*They laugh more heartily.*)

HENRY

Who in our brood has ever committed marriage?

JOHN

Mama and Papa.

HENRY

Only legally. Except for a couple of slips that brought about you and
me, Papa is pure bachelor and Mama is a living pillar of spinsterhood.
Thanks to your courageous inaction, the Thoreaus remain a race of
maiden aunts and bachelors. All of us, December Virgins!

JOHN

Henry, I never told you about one April——
(HENRY *lifts one hand in mock forgiveness.*)

HENRY

Boy, if Father can falter, so can you!
(*They laugh together, then grow serious.*)

JOHN

It makes for a rather lonely-looking future.

HENRY

Lonely? Never! Why, when I'm ninety and you're a mere infant of
eighty-eight, you'll come around and comfort me.

JOHN

When you're ninety, Henry, I'll be a "mere infant" of ninety-two.

45

(HENRY *grasps his brother's hand.*)

HENRY

And *that's* the time we'll *both* go after the hand of Ellen Sewell!

(HENRY *and* JOHN *leap about, laughing, as if they were a pair of nonagenarians who have been injected with "youth-juice." Then they fall into each other's arms, laughing helplessly.*

The light goes black. In utter darkness, the church-bell tolls mournfully. Dimly the stained glass window of the church appears. Then a cold white spot, directly above, strikes the box which was *the boat and has now been turned over to become a coffin.*)

VOICE OF MINISTER

Unto Almighty God we commend the soul of our brother departed, John Thoreau, and we commit his body to the ground, in the sure and certain hope of the Resurrection unto Eternal Life. Let us pray.

(*Four black-coated townspeople carry off the casket. The* MOTHER *is in black.* HENRY *comes slowly to her side. She looks into his face.*)

MOTHER

David Henry. *Pray* with me!

(MOTHER *kneels, facing front. Almost like a sleep-walker,* HENRY *sinks to his knees. His face is mask-like. His* MOTHER *clasps her hands. Automatically* HENRY *does the same.*)

MOTHER (*With difficulty.*)

Our Father, which art in Heaven, hallowed be——

(*She breaks off, looks at her silent son, who has lowered his hands.*)

HENRY

I can't, Mother. I can't pray.

MOTHER

It helps.

HENRY

Does it? I prayed *before*. What good did it do?

MOTHER

We should pray for John's soul.

HENRY

John's soul can take care of itself.

MOTHER

We should pray for understanding——

46

(HENRY *suddenly gets up, angrily.*)

HENRY

I understand! God has stopped listening, Mother—if He ever *did* listen. What kind of God would fail to see the godliness in John? I can't pray to Him.

(HENRY *turns away, then comes back, kisses his* MOTHER'*s head. Quietly:*)

Mother. Pray for *both* your sons.

(*The* MOTHER *lowers her head, praying as she moves off. The stained-glass projection fades.* ELLEN *hurries on.*)

ELLEN (*Sympathetically.*)

What happened?

HENRY (*Shrugs.*)

He died.

ELLEN

I was in Winthrop. I didn't even hear about it until after the funeral. . . .

HENRY

We managed.

ELLEN

How did—didn't anybody know, beforehand——?

HENRY

What do you want, a medical report? To feed a morbid curiosity?

ELLEN

Even though I couldn't marry him——

HENRY

Couldn't you? Well, that's your business.

ELLEN

Henry, don't be so selfish with your sorrow! *I care too!*

HENRY

He had a glamorous death. Like the Knights of the Table Round who slashed at each other with rusty swords until they had all died of blood-poisoning.

ELLEN

I don't understand.

47

HENRY

John, three mornings ago, happened to think of something very funny
while he was shaving. He burst out laughing, and cut himself. The
razor was old, and vicious, and it despised the blood in his veins. And
so—

(*Confronting her fiercely.*)

—would you like the details? The spasms, the retching, the murderous
ineptitude of doctors, the paralysis of the tongue, the choking, the
clamping of the jaw, the blood-black face, the eyes pleading for oxygen,
the——

(HENRY *suddenly is seized with the symptoms of psychosomatic lock-
jaw, and seems to be going through his brother's agony.*)

ELLEN (*Aghast.*)

Henry!

(*He overcomes the illusion, breathes heavily, gets control of himself.*)

HENRY (*Depleted, but intensely.*)

If a lightning bolt had struck him, that might have been worthy of the
size of the man. But a nick in the finger from a dull razor—what
an indignity! What kind of God would drain away such youth and
energy and laughter! A sneak attack from the Almighty.

(*Turning his face to the sky.*)

You plagued Job, but you spared him! Why couldn't you have been
as fair with John?

(ELLEN *moves toward him, wants to touch him, to comfort him—but
she doesn't.*)

ELLEN

I wonder if—if God lets us be hurt—so we can learn to *transcend* the
pain . . . ?

(*She speaks very softly and simply.*)

In the boat, I didn't understand, really. But is it possible, Henry, that
—even though he's stopped *living,* John continues to *be?*

(HENRY *turns and looks at her. She did* understand! *There is a strong
urge in* HENRY *to embrace her; but a stronger reserve, which prevents
him.*

The light falls away on them. Another light picks up WALDO, *seated,
presumably in his study.* LYDIAN *stands behind him.* HENRY *shifts his*

weight from one foot to the other as WALDO *studies him thoughtfully.*)

WALDO

Well, what sort of work would you like to do?

HENRY

Anything. I wish to use my hands.

WALDO

And what about your head?

HENRY

It could be useful. For burrowing, perhaps.

(LYDIAN *laughs.*)

I could beat it into a ploughshare. It might be a better tool than it's been for thinking.

WALDO

You're giving up *thinking?*

HENRY

For this lifetime, yes.

WALDO (*Turning to his wife.*)

We could certainly use a handyman, Lydian.

(*To* HENRY.)

Mrs. Emerson will assure you that, of all God's creatures, I am the least handy of men. My skill at carpentry stops at cutting cheese.

(*They laugh,* HENRY *a bit uneasily.*)

LYDIAN

There's a great deal that needs doing. The wall by the back meadow needs mending.

HENRY

I am a mason.

WALDO

You are?

HENRY (*Quickly.*)

No, of course I'm not a *Mason*—but I *do* masonry.

WALDO

The weeds are at war with the marigolds. And the last time I looked, the weeds were winning.

HENRY

They're doomed. Being a weed myself, I infiltrate their ranks.

49

WALDO

What about children, Mr. Thoreau?

HENRY

What about them?

LYDIAN

You've had experience with them?

HENRY

Well, I was a child once myself. Briefly.

LYDIAN (*To* WALDO.)

It would be so good for Edward—to have someone who could take him boating and hiking. . . .

(*To* HENRY.)

Dr. Emerson has so little time to be a father—he's so occupied with his lectures and writing.

HENRY

When I'm with your son, Dr. Emerson, I might turn my brain back on —temporarily.

WALDO

I think this might prove to be a very good arrangement. Of course, there's the matter of compensation.

HENRY

I've been paid.

(WALDO *lifts his eyebrows, puzzled.*)

With something far more extraordinary than money. And more valuable. The words you fling into an audience from the lecture platform —you never know what happens to them, do you? No more than a Roman Emperor knew what happened to the coins he scattered to the crowd as he rode through the streets.

WALDO

The Roman Emperors were trying to buy popularity.

HENRY

And the poor fellows only had gold. No wonder Rome fell!

(*Growing more intense.*)

But I sat on the grass at Harvard Yard and heard you speak for the first time. I was at the very edge of the assembly—but I think I caught more coins than the crowd at the wheels of your chariot.

50

WALDO (*To* LYDIAN.)

This may be interesting, having a Harvard man as a handyman.

(*To* HENRY.)

I'm vain, you know. Of necessity. I'm not as lucky as the Caesars; I have to mint all my own coins. So a man sits at his desk and doubts constantly: is it gold or is it tin?

HENRY

I apologize. It was a faulty metaphor. Money is merely money. You can never spend a thought. It still belongs to you—though it makes other men rich!

WALDO (*Accusingly.*)

You're thinking, Mr. Thoreau. Incidentally, if we're going to have you around here—you, and your hands, and your head—I can't possibly go on calling you "Mr. Thoreau." Your mother calls you "David," I believe?

HENRY

I call myself "Henry."

WALDO (*Drily.*)

My mother called *me* "Ralph." You may call me "Waldo."

(*They laugh and shake hands.*)

And Lydian, of course, is "Lydian." And Edward—where's Edward?

(*Calls.*)

Edward!

LYDIAN

It's important, I think, for you to meet Edward. To be sure that you two are . . . companionable.

WALDO

Why shouldn't they be?

(EDWARD *comes on. He is eight, and has the shyness and reserve of the son of a famous father.*)

EDWARD (*Reporting to his father.*)

Yes, sir?

WALDO

A firm handshake, Edward, for Mr. Thoreau.

(EDWARD *and* HENRY *shake hands.*)

You're going to be extremely good friends.

51

HENRY (*Easily, but not glibly.*)

I don't see why not.

EDWARD (*Stiffly.*)

How do you do, sir.

(EDWARD *is cautious in his friendships.*)

LYDIAN

Isn't it nice, Edward—having a new member of the family?

EDWARD (*Obediently.*)

Yes, ma'am.

LYDIAN (*To her husband.*)

But we can't expect Henry to work for the same munificent salary we pay Edward—which is nothing.

WALDO

Not true. Every Saturday morning, wet or fair, Edward gets a shiny new dime.

EDWARD (*Surprised.*)

I do?

WALDO

Which I promptly put in the bank for him.

LYDIAN (*With a faint smile.*)

Some weeks he's overpaid.

(*The boy laughs—and it is clear that he is more at ease with his mother than with his father.*)

WALDO (*Dismissing the boy, rather automatically.*)

That will be all, Edward. Back to your studies.

EDWARD

Yes, Father.

(*The boys scoots off.*)

HENRY (*Watching the boy go.*)

If it will make you feel better, I'll take the same pay as Edward—and try to be worth it.

WALDO

Henry, you're not a very good businessman.

HENRY

I'm not a businessman at all. If you don't pay me a regular salary, then I won't feel obliged to keep regular hours. I love a broad margin to my life . . .

52

(*Quickly.*)
But I assure you, the work will be done.

WALDO

Then you must have weekly wages . . .

HENRY

But must it be *money?* Could it be—
(*He breaks off. There is a soft, leafy-green projection and the distant music of a flute.* HENRY *pauses to hear it.* WALDO *and* LYDIAN *stare at him strangely, as he stares way off, toward Walden, far in the back of the auditorium or beyond.*)
How far does it extend, your back meadow?

WALDO

To the woods.

HENRY

Including the woods?

WALDO

A section of it. To the shore of the pond.
(*The flute music rises, accelerates: the idea is accelerating inside his head.*)

HENRY

Perhaps, some day, if my work has been useful to you, and if we remain friends, I may ask you for a bit of your woods——
(*Quickly.*)
A small square, no bigger than this room. Not as a gift, I don't want to own it! Simply an understanding between friends—who know that the land really belongs to the woodchucks, anyhow!

LYDIAN

What will you do with it?

HENRY

I'm not quite sure. It's an idea I have . . . an "experiment" . . .
(*The flute melody lingers, then falls away, as does the leafy projection.*)

WALDO

Good thinking, Henry. You're planning 'way up ahead, for your retirement.

HENRY

Retirement? What an absurd idea! Why spend the best part of your

53

life earning money so that you can enjoy a questionable liberty during the least valuable part of it? Why work like a dog so you can pant for a moment or two before you die?

(WALDO *laughs.*)

WALDO

Carlyle told me about an Englishman who went off to India—"Injah," he called it—to make a huge fortune so that he could come back to the Lake Country and live the life of a poet.

HENRY

If there was a poem in him, he should have rushed straight up to his garret.

WALDO

He should have! He died in the Punjab—immensely wealthy, but without a sonnet to his name.

LYDIAN

Can Henry have his parcel of woods? For his "experiment"?

WALDO

Well, I don't know what kind of experiment you have in mind. But if the woodchucks don't object, why should I?

HENRY

Thank you, Doctor—uh—

(*Corrects himself.*)

—Waldo.

WALDO (*To his wife.*)

I don't really have time to make a list of all the things that need doing. Lydian, could you go into the details with Henry—various things that—

HENRY

Don't make a list. *Things* will tell me what needs to be done.

WALDO

Oh, what a relief! The hell of having people help you is that they are constantly completing what you gave them to do—and they come knocking on your door, saying: "What shall I do next?" Always when you are in the midst of doing what you your*self* should be doing next!

HENRY

I respect a man's privacy. I'll never knock at the door of your study.

WALDO

Don't be too much a stranger, Henry. Uh—I might interrupt *your* work now and then—and ask you to help me mend a cracked wall or pull a few weeds in a lecture I'm writing.

HENRY

I'm not a polite man. I'll be as frank with you as I am with the back meadow.

(HENRY *leaves.* LYDIAN *and* WALDO *stare after him.*)

LYDIAN

Not many people will understand that young man. He doesn't want anything.

WALDO

Perhaps he wants too much.

(*All light falls away, except the moonlight glow on the jail cell.* HENRY *walks back into the cell, stands by the barred casement and listens again to the sounds of Concord.* BAILEY *jerks awake, sits up suddenly.*)

BAILEY

What time is it?

HENRY

Where were you planning to go?

BAILEY

Back to sleep. But I like to know how much of the night has swum by.

HENRY

In Samarkand, it is not quite noon.

BAILEY

That near Boston?

HENRY

It's as far away from Boston as you can get—before you start coming *back* to Boston again.

BAILEY

I never could figger out how it could be *one* time here and *another* time somewheres else. Isn't it *now* all over?

HENRY

You're wiser than most men who wear watches. I don't know what good it does to hang numbers on the hours. You can't count a river while it moves by you. The best thing to do is take off your clothes and go swimming in it. And when you feel the water all around you, then you're part of the total river—where it's been, where it is, where it's flowing. Plunge in!

BAILEY

I don't swim good.

HENRY

There's no trick to it. Yes, there is. One trick. You can't struggle with the water. If you fling your arms around and thrash and fight the stream, it fights back. And you go under.

(*A drunk, laughing incoherently, staggers across the thrust, a mug of ale still in his hand. He drains the mug, thrashes about wildly.* BAILEY *rises from his cot, crosses to the window beside* THOREAU. *They both look out.*)

BAILEY

That one's gone pretty far under.

(*With the broken melody of a drinking song, the drunk weaves off.*)

HENRY

Drowned and drunk with ale and civilization.

BAILEY

Do you drink?

HENRY

Do you?

BAILEY

When I can afford it.

HENRY

It doesn't cost anything to be drunk. It needn't. It shouldn't. A man can be drunk all the time. Where I live, you can get drunk on the air.

BAILEY (*Deliciously intrigued.*)

Where's that? When they let me out, maybe I'll come get drunk with you. When they let *you* out. Where's it at?

HENRY

In the woods. By a pond.

(*The flute melody drifts in with a leafy-green projection.*)

BAILEY

Away from everything?

56

HENRY

Oh, where I live, I have a great deal of company. But no people.

BAILEY

Don't you get scared? At night—in the dark?

HENRY

Why be afraid? The witches are all hung. Christianity and candles have been invented.

BAILEY

You live there all the time?

HENRY

All the time.

BAILEY (*Wistfully.*)

I wish I had a place to *belong.* It's always been a marvel to me how a man can git the money together to own himself a house that belongs to *him.*

HENRY

Want to hear how much my mansion cost me? Twenty-eight dollars, twelve and a half cents!

BAILEY

Man-a-mighty! I alwuz thought a house cost a fortune. Hundred dollars or more! How do you eat?

HENRY

Very well. I have a bean patch, some Indian corn. Now and then Walden serves me up a fish.

BAILEY

What happens in winter?

HENRY (*Starting to take off one shoe.*)

It snows. So I don't even have to go to the pond for fresh water—just reach out the door for a handful of snow. Melt it, and it's sweet as the sky.

(*Flute and woods projection fade.*)

Oh, there are a few things you have to get in town. So you walk into town.

(**HENRY** *pulls off his shoe, thrusts his hand into it and pokes his finger through a hole in the sole. Then, one shoe on and one shoe off, he*

57

comes into the foreground. The light subsides on the jail cell and BAILEY *lies back on his cot in the shadows.*

It is late afternoon of a hot July day, and the thrust is the main street of Concord. Several people pass by HENRY. *They look questioningly at his curious condition; one shoe on and one shoe off. But* HENRY *seems oblivious to it. He nods, saluting the passers-by with his shoe.* DEACON BALL *comes by, looks at* HENRY *disdainfully.*)

BALL

You've condescended to pay a call on civilization, Mr. Thoreau?

HENRY

Briefly. And reluctantly.

BALL

How is life among the savages?

HENRY

If I'm in Concord long enough, Deacon, I may find out.

(*Blithely,* HENRY *salutes him with his shoe and limps on.* SAM STAPLES *ambles toward* HENRY. *He has a piece of paper which he holds distastefully.*)

SAM (*Clearing his throat.*)

Hullo, Henry.

HENRY

Oh, hello, Sam.

SAM

What's wrong with your foot?

HENRY

Foot's fine. Got a sick shoe.

(*He wiggles a finger through the hole in the sole.*)

Cobbler'll cure it.

(HENRY *starts to walk down the street.*)

SAM

Henry. I—uh—got something here for ya.

HENRY

Oh?

SAM (*Awkwardly.*)

I can understand how a man could forget—bein' as busy as you are—out there—uh—writin' about them birds and talkin' to the fish and whatever else it is you do out there by yourself. Naturally it don't occur to you to think much about *taxes.*

HENRY

No, I don't think much of taxes.

SAM

But they gotta be paid.

HENRY

Why?

SAM

It's the law. I ain't blamin' you for bein' forgetful, Henry. May surprise you to learn you ain't paid your tax for two years.

HENRY

Six.

SAM *(Firming up.)*

I got this order. And I got to serve it on ya. Here!
(He thrusts the legal paper on HENRY.)
HENRY *(With a kind of arrogant calm.)*

Why, thanks, Sam.
(He takes the document, glances at it, then folds it slowly, creasing it carefully. Then he slides it inside his shoe and pulls the shoe on. He stands on it, tests it with a few steps.)
Fits just fine! Exactly what I needed. I may not have to go to the cobbler after all.

SAM *(Irked.)*

Now, Henry. That there is an official paper. You can't walk over it like that.

HENRY

Why not? Best thing I ever got from the government. Most practical, anyhow.

SAM

Look, it don't pleasure me none, servin' a court order on you. Sometimes this is an unpleasant job!

HENRY

Then quit. If you don't like bein' constable, Sam, resign.

SAM

Somebody's got to do the work of the people.

HENRY

Oh, you work for the people?

SAM

Yes!

HENRY

Well, I'm "people"—and you don't have to work for me. You're *free!*
If it'll make you any happier, I'll fire you!

SAM

Lookee here, Henry. You gonna pay up your tax or ain't ya?

HENRY

You pay *your* tax, Sam?

SAM

If I didn't, I'd have to arrest myself.

HENRY

Are you going to arrest *me?*
(*There's a long pause. The two men look at each other evenly.*)

SAM

I don't *want* to, Henry. But the government gets persnickety about
taxes when we got a war goin'.
(*Quietly, the blood is beginning to boil within* HENRY.)
After all, it ain't a big sum of money. If—if you're hard up, why *I'll*
pay it.

HENRY (*Erupting.*)

Don't you dare!

SAM

A loan, just. You can pay me back when—
(*Now all the molten outrage within* HENRY DAVID THOREAU *bursts out
like lava from a live volcano.*)

HENRY

I will not pay one copper penny to an unjust government! I wouldn't
pay the tithe and tariff to the church, so I signed off from the church!
Well, I'm ready right now, Sam, to sign off from the government.
Where do I sign? Where?

SAM

You can't do that.

60

HENRY
Why not?

SAM (*Lamely.*)
Well, even the President has to obey the laws!

HENRY
The poor President! What with preserving his popularity and doing his duty, he doesn't know what to do.

SAM
If the majority says——

HENRY
I'm the majority. A majority of one!

BALL (*From the edge of the crowd.*)
Arrest him!

SAM (*Plaintively.*)
I don't want to arrest him—

HENRY
Go ahead, Constable. An honest man can't come into town to have his shoes fixed. Not even a pair—one shoe—
(*He tugs the shoe off his foot, yanks the paper out from inside and brandishes it.*)
—without his neighbors coming around to *paw* him with their dirty institutions.
(*For the first time,* HENRY *realizes that he is surrounded by a little ring of people, so he addresses them as well as* SAM.)
I'll tell you this. If one thousand . . . If one hundred . . . If ten men . . . ten honest men, only . . . If *one* honest man in this state of Massachusetts had the conviction and the courage to withdraw from this unholy partnership and let himself be locked up in the County Jail, it'd be the start of more true freedom than we've seen since a few farmers had the guts to block the British by the bridge up the road.
(*He points off.*)

ANOTHER VOICE
Lawbreaker!

HENRY
What law ever made men free? Men have got to make the *law* free.

61

And if a law is wrong, by Heaven, it's the duty of a man to stand up and say so. Even if your oddfellow society wants to clap him in a jail.

FARMER

That's revolution!

HENRY

Yes, sir, that's revolution! What do you think happened at Concord Bridge? A prayer meeting?
(*Pointing again, emphatically.*)

SAM

What are you tryin' to do, Henry? Wipe out all the laws?

HENRY

As many as possible.

FARMER

What's the whole stew about?

SAM

He don't want to pay his tax.

FARMER

Neither do I.

SAM (*Pointing to* HENRY.)

Yeah, but he ain't payin' his.

FARMER

Henry, it would upset your Maw if you run amuck ag'in society.

HENRY

Society's "run amuck" against *me*. I'm just going to the cobbler, minding my own business. I ask nothing from the government. Why should it take from me?

BALL

Throw him in jail!

HENRY

What're you waiting for, Sam? Get out the chains. Drag me off to jail.

SAM

There must be somethin' almighty wrong when a man's so willing to go!

HENRY

Sam. It's very simple. What the government of this country is doing *turns my stomach!* And if I keep my mouth shut, I'm a criminal. To my Conscience. To my God. To Society. And to *you*, Sam Staples. You want a dollar from me? If I don't approve the way that dollar's spent, you're not going to get it!

SAM

I swear I can't figger what makes you so ornery, Henry.

HENRY

Have you heard what they're doing down in Washington?

SAM

I—well, I don't have much time for newspapers. And I read slow.

HENRY

Open up your ears, then. Find out what he's up to—your Hired Man in the White House.

SAM

He's not just *my* President; he's yours, too.

HENRY

No, sir. I'm not paying his salary. He's fired!

SAM

You think high of Dr. Emerson, don't you?

HENRY

Usually.

SAM

He's paid his tax.

HENRY

That's his problem. I'm not paying mine.

SAM

All I know is, it ain't fittin' to throw a Harvard Man in jail. 'Specially a Thoreau. A honester man than you, Henry, I never knew.

HENRY

Is that a compliment, Sam?

SAM

Yes, sir.

HENRY

Well, thanks. Now clap me in your Bastille.

(HENRY *puts out his hands to be manacled.* SAM *sighs, looks around at the little cluster of townsmen. He shrugs helplessly, then leads* HENRY *off. There is a shocked pause.*)

63

FARMER

Somebody better go tell his Maw.

WOMAN

But don't let his Aunt Louisa know; she'll have a conniption fit.
(*Thinks—then with relish.*)
I'm gonna go tell her!
(*She hurries off. The cluster dissipates in various directions, and the
light in the foreground falls away.*

HENRY *and* SAM *come into the cell.* BAILEY *is on the cot, covered by a
blanket.* HENRY *doesn't realize at first that he has a cellmate.* SAM *car-
ries a ring of keys, which he tosses on the bed, and a well-worn ledger
book.* HENRY *looks around.*)

SAM

Ain't much, but it's clean.
(BAILEY *emits a loud snore.*)

HENRY

Music, too. Very soothing.

SAM

(*As he wets the stub of pencil in his mouth.*)
Now, Henry, I gotta put down your age.

HENRY

Twenty-nine summers.

SAM (*Writing painfully.*)

Two-nine. Occupation?

HENRY

What do you need that for, Sam?

SAM

If I don't fill this all out correct, the Selectmen don't pay your board.

HENRY (*Nodding toward the sleeper.*)

What's *his* occupation?

SAM

Him? He's a vagrant.

HENRY

So am I.

SAM (*Unhappy about the whole thing.*)

Henry, that's no occupation. That's another charge! Gimme somethin'
to put down. What *are* you, exactly?

64

HENRY

What am I?

(*Thinking.*)

Oh, Ho-er of Beans. Fisherman. Inspector of Snowstorms . . .

SAM (*Impatiently.*)

Them won't do.

HENRY

You want *respectable* trades? Let's see. Pencil-maker—occasionally. Schoolteacher—once. Surveyor. Carpenter. Author—alleged. Huckleberry-hunter—expert . . .

SAM (*Writing.*)

Carpenter. That'll do.

HENRY

Risky, Sam. You'll shock the clergy if you lock up a carpenter.

SAM

(*After a little thought.*)

It's writ.

(*He slaps his ledger book shut and goes off, shaking his head. The lighting in the cell slowly, imperceptibly, turns into night.*

There is the urgent jangling of a bell-pull. The lights rise on the EMERSON *area.* LYDIAN *appears in a night-robe. She is reading a note— puzzled and concerned.*)

WALDO'S VOICE (*From off.*)

Who is it? I'll get it.

LYDIAN

I already have, dear.

(WALDO *comes on in nightdress, wearing a nightcap.*)

WALDO (*Sleepily.*)

I'll get it. I've got it. Oh, Lydian—what are you doing up?

LYDIAN

(*To* WALDO, *indicating the note.*)

It's about Henry. He's in jail.

WALDO

God help us! Why? What did he do?

LYDIAN

It isn't clear——

WALDO

He murdered Deacon Ball! One of Henry's acts of mercy.

LYDIAN

No——

WALDO

They've found Deacon Ball murdered, and they're accusing Henry!

LYDIAN

Deacon Ball hasn't been murdered.

WALDO

Oh? That's too bad. Let me look at that.

(*She hands him the note. Simultaneously, the light rises on* MRS. THOREAU, *distraught.*)

MOTHER

Every night, Louisa. Every night I have this terrible nightmare. I dream that David Henry is in jail. But tonight I didn't even have to go to sleep!

(*The light on* MRS. THOREAU *fades. In the cell,* SAM *re-enters, standing at the cell door.*)

SAM

Before I take my boots off for the night, Henry, why don't you pay up an' let me let you outa here?

HENRY (*Gently.*)

Take off your boots, Sam.

(SAM *still hesitates. In the* EMERSON *area,* WALDO *grows fully awake.*)

WALDO

Lydian. I've got to get on my boots. Where's my coat? I've got to go down to Concord Square—!

(*He sits, pulling on a pair of high-topped shoes over his naked feet.* LYDIAN *hands him a black topcoat, which he puts on over his nightshirt.*)

LYDIAN

You're going to go like that?

WALDO

That boy's in trouble!

(*He starts out.* LYDIAN *quickly pulls off his nightcap as* WALDO *hurries off. The light in the* EMERSON *area fades.*)

66

SAM (*Pleading.*)

Please pay up, Henry.

(*Previously,* HENRY *has been volcanic. Now the lava has cooled but firmed.*)

HENRY

If you call on me to pay for a rifle, Sam, it's the same as asking me to fire it! You're making me as much a killer as the foot-soldier who crashes across the border into faraway Mexico, charges into his neighbor's house, sets fire to it and kills his children!

(*The two men study each other. Troubled,* SAM *starts to leave.* HENRY *goes to the cot, calls.*)

Sam!

(SAM *races back eagerly, thinking* HENRY *may have changed his mind.*)

You forgot your keys.

(*He hands* SAM *the ring of keys.*)

SAM (*Disappointed.*)

Oh.

(*He takes them, goes out, locks the door.* HENRY *stares through the bars, listening to the night silence of the village. From the back of the theatre, as if shouting across Concord Square, a voice breaks the quiet.*)

WALDO

Henry! *Henry!* What are you doing in jail?

(HENRY *turns, faces front, responding to the challenge.*)

HENRY

(*Defiantly, pointing accusingly across Concord Square*)

Waldo! What are you doing *out* of jail?

(*The lights fade.*)

Act Two

(The light rises on the jail cell—moonlight casting shadows through the bars at a later angle. No light falls on either cot, but on the space between them. The town clock strikes two. The dim light gradually reveals the forms of the two men, each motionless, seemingly asleep. HENRY *stirs, coughs, gets up restlessly, paces a few times, goes to the barred casement. His hand reaches up in the white clarity of the moonlight. He touches the bars. Then, with a musical fancy, he pretends to pluck each bar as if it were a harp-string.)*

HENRY *(Imitating the sound of a harp-string.)*
Ting . . . ting . . . ting . . . tang.
(He riffles the bars as if he were doing arpeggios, which he vocalizes idly. Stops suddenly, looks toward his cellmate.)
In the prison of heaven, that's how the angels make music.
(He paces.)
I am told.
(Paces some more.)
Not having been there.
(Paces more.)
And not likely to be invited.
*(*HENRY *sits on his own cot and talks to the sleeping* BAILEY.*)*
You know what the government said to me, Bailey? "Your money or your life." I won't give it my money. And they think they have my life!
(Laughs a little.)
Only my body. I'm a free man. Free to touch my nose if I like.
(He touches his nose.)
Or not.
(He takes his hand down.)
Free to stand. Or not to stand. They can't lock up my thoughts! What I *believe* goes easily through these walls—as if the stones were air.

(He gestures front—where the wall, in fact, does not exist.)

The state is so afraid of us, Bailey, that it locks us up. The state is timid as a lone woman with her silver spoons! We have frightened her out of her wits.

(The light comes up on LYDIAN.)

LYDIAN

Henry, you have wits enough to know that, in order to *get* along, you have to *go* along!

(HENRY the volcano erupts again.)

HENRY *(Shouting, contemptuously.)*

GO ALONG! GO ALONG! GO ALONG!

(LYDIAN has reached for a little straw berry-basket.)

LYDIAN

Edward?

(The little boy comes running to her.)

Go along with Mr. Thoreau.

EDWARD

Where are we going?

(HENRY saunters down from the cell onto the thrust. Rakishly he puts on the wide-brimmed straw hat which he wore before. The thrust becomes a sunny meadow.)

HENRY

Huckleberry-hunting, my boy! Would you like to study composition with Mozart? Painting with Michelangelo? Study huckleberry-hunting with Thoreau, it's the same thing!

(EDWARD laughs; LYDIAN slips off as the huckleberry-hunters parade through the sun-drenched field.)

Now, when *I* was your age—if I was ever your age—my mother used to bake huckleberry pudding. Best in Concord. But all my Mama and my Papa and Uncle Charlie and Aunt Louisa and my brother John got—all *they* got—was the pudding. I had the glory of discovering the huckleberries! A half-day of wild adventure under the Concord sky.

EDWARD

How do you find huckleberries? *I* want to discover some!

HENRY *(Imparting a great secret.)*

Huckleberries are very difficult to find. Because most people think that . . . they're over *there!*

72

(He makes a dramatic gesture.)

EDWARD

Should I go over there?

HENRY

No, sir! The *best* huckleberries have a sly way . . . of being . . . exactly . . . where . . . you . . . are . . . standing! Here!
(He bends down quickly, picks an imaginary huckleberry.)
The trick of it is: you have to know where to stand!

EDWARD *(Plucking one.)*

Can I taste one? Right now?

HENRY *(Thinking.)*

Well . . . yes. But for every one you taste, you have to take *two* home.

EDWARD *(Tasting.)*

Mmmmm . . . They're good! Where's your basket?

HENRY

I use my hat. Since my head is precisely the size of a huckleberry pudding!
(EDWARD runs about, seeming to gather huckleberries.)

EDWARD *(Shouts.)*

Here's a whole patch of them!

HENRY

Ahhh, you have talent—no doubt about it.

EDWARD *(Running from bush to bush.)*

Let's race and see who can get the most first.
(But HENRY is no racer. He has paused to savor a particular berry.)

HENRY *(Swallowing, benignly.)*

That was a happy huckleberry!
(Little EDWARD is plunging about, grasping handfuls of huckleberries as fast as he can.)

EDWARD

Look! I've got more than you have!

HENRY

Everybody does.
(With deliberate relaxation, HENRY is plucking the berries, tossing, them in his hat. His ease and calm is in contrast with the boy's bounding energy. HENRY seems to be choosing the precise berry at each bush —the one which promises the best flavor.)

73

EDWARD

How does a huckleberry get to be a huckleberry instead of a strawberry?

HENRY

Well, there are a number of books on the subject. But *meeting* a huckleberry makes you more of an expert than any botanist who ever wrote a dull book.

(*Now* EDWARD *has completely filled his basket, and comes running joyfully to* HENRY, *to show him.*)

EDWARD

Look! Look, Henry! Mine's all the way to the top. Mama should've given me a bigger basket!

(*Suddenly the running boy trips, falls—and the whole basket of berries—imaginary—spills out over the ground.* EDWARD *is aghast at the accident. His bright-eyed ecstasy turns to tears.*)

They're all spilled and spoiled!

(HENRY *drops to his knees, puts his arm around the shoulders of the dejected boy, who sobs uncontrollably.*)

HENRY

Don't you know what you've done? You have planted whole patches of huckleberries, for an entire generation of Edward Emersons!

EDWARD

I have . . . ?
(*Through his subsiding tears.*)
How?

HENRY

Because that's the way things are: Nature has provided that little boys gathering huckleberries should, now and then, stumble and scatter the berries. Edward, you have been as helpful as a honey-bee!

EDWARD (*Now delighted.*)

Let's pick some more—and *spill* 'em!
(*With a grin,* EDWARD *wipes his sleeve across his eyes, reversing his previous misery.* HENRY *pours his hatful of huckleberries into Edward's basket.* EDWARD *looks up into his face.*)
But those are yours . . . !

HENRY (*Solemnly.*)

I surrender title.

EDWARD

What does that mean?

HENRY

Like most of the voodoo of ownership, it means absolutely nothing.
(*The boy takes* HENRY's *hand.*)

EDWARD

Henry. I wish you were my father . . . !
(HENRY *looks at the boy, wishing he were, too, but not saying it. The
lighting fades on them and simultaneously rises on* LYDIAN, *who is
seated, writing a letter. She looks up as* HENRY *and* EDWARD *walk into
the* EMERSON *area.* EDWARD *swings his basket of borrowed huckleberries
. . . but carefully!*)

EDWARD (*Running to his mother.*)

These are for you, Mama!
(*And he gives the basket to* LYDIAN.)

LYDIAN

My, what a present! Thank you, Edward.

EDWARD

(*The honesty forcing it out of him.*)
I guess—really—you should thank Henry.

LYDIAN (*Correcting him.*)

Mr. Thoreau, dear.

EDWARD

Henry says I should call him "Henry."

HENRY

There's not too much formality in the huckleberry-hunting business.
(*They laugh a little.*)

EDWARD

And, Mama. I've asked Henry to be my father.
(LYDIAN *and* HENRY *look at each other.* HENRY *shrugs, a bit embar-
rassed.*)

LYDIAN

Oh? What about your real father?

75

EDWARD

He's never here. He's always 'way on the other side of the ocean, or out somewhere making speeches, or up in his room where I can't disturb him. But Henry—

(*A pause.*)

HENRY

—is here.

(LYDIAN *hesitates, then hands the basket back to* EDWARD.)

LYDIAN

Take your huckleberries to the kitchen, will you, dear?

(*The boy starts off, then turns, at the edge of the light.*)

EDWARD (*With a fresh thought.*)

If Henry's my father, that means you've got a husband, Mama. Not in England or someplace else all the time, but right here in our house. Wouldn't that be nicer? For you?

(LYDIAN *and* HENRY *exchange glances, and the boy goes off.*)

LYDIAN

I—I suppose it isn't wise. For you to keep on working here while Waldo's away.

HENRY

Please don't be afraid of me . . .

LYDIAN

Shouldn't I be?

(*She gets up, restlessly.*)

Oh, you're going to tell me that you have too much respect. For the Sage of Concord.

HENRY

And his wife.

LYDIAN

Respect is based on friendship. And friendship is based on love. And love is so . . . accidental. Isn't it, Henry?

(HENRY *moistens his lips.*)

HENRY

We love without knowing it. A man—or a woman—can't love on schedule. I don't wake up in the morning and say: "I shall start loving at nine-twenty, and continue until ten-fifteen." Yes, it *is* accidental. And it's everywhere—it's the wind, the tide, the waves, the sunshine.

LYDIAN (*Very quietly.*)

Henry. If love is all around you, like huckleberries—why do you pick loneliness?

(EDWARD *bursts in carrying a protesting live chicken.*)

EDWARD

Mama! Henry! Look what happened to the chicken's feet!

(*The boy holds up the chicken.*)

He's wearing gloves!

LYDIAN

No, Edward, that's not poss—it *is* wearing gloves!

(*She turns, puzzled, to* HENRY.)

HENRY (*A little sheepishly.*)

The other day you said they were scratching in your garden, uprooting your rose plants. So I gave a little elegance to the ladies of the henhouse. They've scratched their last. Your roses are safe.

LYDIAN (*Examining the chicken-gloves.*)

You made these for all the chickens?

HENRY

I'm opposed to social distinctions. Once one chicken is gloved, you can't expect the other ladies to go about bare-clawed.

(*They laugh.*)

EDWARD (*Eagerly.*)

Can I take him out and show him to everybody?

LYDIAN

He's a "she," dear. Yes, I suppose you can.

HENRY

But bring the lady home and latch the gate. If you want an omelette for breakfast.

(EDWARD *scurries off with the chicken.*)

LYDIAN

My roses thank you.

HENRY

Oh, they're very welcome.

LYDIAN

Get married, Henry. Find a face—and teach yourself to love it.

HENRY

I have.

(LYDIAN *looks at him quizzically.*)

But I'm a crusty and resolute bachelor. And Nature is my mother-in-law.

LYDIAN

There are so many pretty young girls——

HENRY

I would drive them promptly into old age. I'm not that cruel.

LYDIAN

You need a brain to toss on the pillow next to you. What about Margaret Fuller?

(HENRY *repeats the name, as if he were rinsing it out of his mouth.*)

HENRY

Margaret . . . Fuller . . . ? Oh, I couldn't marry her.

LYDIAN

Why not?

HENRY

Two reasons. First, I'm not stupid enough to ask her. Second, *she'd* never be stupid enough to accept.

(*Turning.*)

You want to be a matchmaker, Lydian? Find me something innocent and natural and uncomplicated. A shrub-oak. A cloud. A leaf lost in the snow.

LYDIAN

But isn't it lonely, Henry?

HENRY

Lonely!

(*He laughs.*)

I am no more lonely, Lydian, than the North Star, or the South Wind, or the first spider in a new house.

(*Then gently.*)

What about *your* loneliness? Is it enough to go to bed each night with nothing but a letter from England? Telling about your husband's over-whelming passion . . . for Carlyle?

(*She looks down.* HENRY *reaches out, touching her sleeve.*)

Isn't it a pity that you are so "safe" with me?

(*In the cell,* BAILEY *seems in the midst of a conversation.*)

BAILEY

I'm skeered of a trial. I ain't got no lawyer. 'Course the food ain't too bad here.

(HENRY *has crossed back into the cell and the lights have faded on* LYDIAN.)

Would *you* be my lawyer?

HENRY (*Stops short.*)

I'm no lawyer!

BAILEY

Couldn't you be one—for me? You talk like a lawyer. And you're smart as most.

HENRY

Bailey, I would give you my coat, or my shoes, or my last peck of beans; I would chop wood for you, or push a wheelbarrow for you. But I would not stoop to being a lawyer for anyone! I think Lucifer was a lawyer: that's why the Devil still gives advice to Presidents.

BAILEY

Who'm I gonna get?

HENRY

If I were God, Bailey—instead of just a speck of Him—I wouldn't let you die away in the dark.

(BAILEY *is panicky. He gets up from the cot.*)

BAILEY

Tell me what to do!

HENRY (*Rubbing his chin.*)

Well, you might try getting yourself born in a more just and generous age. That's not a very practical suggestion.

(*Another thought.*)

I suppose you could try prayer.

79

BAILEY
I'm not very good at it.

HENRY
Neither am I.

BAILEY
But could you say one for me?

HENRY
Is the Lord so almighty absentminded that He needs a tap on the shoulder—to remind Him that Adam had children?

BAILEY
A prayer couldn't hurt none.

HENRY
All right. Let's send God a telegram.
(*He clasps his hands in semi-solemnity.*)
"Blessed Are the Young,
    For they do not read the President's speeches.
Blessed Are They who never read a newspaper,
    For they shall see Nature and, through her, God.
And Blessed is Bailey, for he's a good fellow
    and deserves better treatment than you've been
    giving him—even though he *is* a man of letters.
Amen."

BAILEY
Amen. Do you think it got through?

HENRY
I wouldn't know. I don't usually pray with words. I prefer a flute.
(*As* BAILEY *sinks back onto his cot, the lights dip in the cell.* HENRY *moves forward into the amber sunlight of the forestage, and the background takes on again the leaf-woven texture of the Walden woods.* HENRY *reaches for a flute and begins to play something strange and peaceful—an unconventional forest idyll. The shadowy figure of a man climbs out of the pit as* HENRY *plays. Crouching, the man creeps through the brush, unseen by* HENRY. *The man is* WILLIAMS, *a black, in dirty, tattered clothes. He is husky but terrified. Still* HENRY *does not notice him, although he thinks he may have been detected—so he darts behind another imaginary bush. With a sigh,* HENRY *puts aside his*

flute and bends down to reach for something on the ground. WILLIAMS
thinks he is going for a gun. He leaps onto the back of the astonished
HENRY, *clamping a huge hand over* HENRY's *mouth.*)

WILLIAMS

You ain't takin' no gun on me!

(*Calmly* HENRY *rotates the handle of the implement he was reaching
for. It is a hoe.* WILLIAMS *relaxes a little, takes his hand off* HENRY's
mouth.)

HENRY

You thought this was a rifle? A rifle's no good for hoeing beans.

(*He is gentle.*)

Mind if I go ahead?

(WILLIAMS *is afraid, uncertain.*)

There isn't a gun within three-quarters of a mile of here.

(HENRY *is unhanded and begins to hoe. The black watches.*)

What can I do for you?

WILLIAMS

I need vittles. Gimme some vittles!

HENRY

Well, sit down, neighbor. It'll take about three weeks for these beans
to come up.

WILLIAMS

By then I'll be sleepin' wi' them beans! I gotta git to Cañada.

HENRY

To where?

WILLIAMS

Cañada. Cañada! North as I kin git! They say the Norther ya git, the
free-er ya git!

HENRY (*As he hoes.*)

There's a quarter loaf of bread inside the hut. Help yourself.

(WILLIAMS *starts to move in the direction* HENRY *has indicated—then
hesitates, turns back.*)

WILLIAMS

You trustin' me to go inside your place? Without you watchin'?

HENRY

Why not?

(WILLIAMS *pauses—then darts into the shadows while* HENRY *placidly hoes his beans. Then he calls toward the off-stage hut:*)
If you want to stay till supper, I'll catch us a fish. What's your name?
(*Almost immediately* WILLIAMS *reappears with a chunk of bread which he chews on ravenously.*)

WILLIAMS (*His mouth full.*)
Williams.

HENRY
I'm Henry Thoreau.
(*He reaches out his hand.* WILLIAMS *marvels—then reaches out tentatively for* HENRY's *handshake, first wiping his hand on his pant-leg.*)
Williams your first name or your last name?

WILLIAMS
It's all my name.
(*Suddenly.*)
But I ain't no slave. I ain't goin' back to bein' no slave. No man gonna take me back.
(*With fire.*)
I *borned* myself two weeks ago.

HENRY
Good for you, Mr. Williams.

WILLIAMS
I belonged to Mr. Williams. I was Mr. Williams' Williams. No more.
(HENRY *studies him.* WILLIAMS *is wary.*)
You gonna turn me in?

HENRY
I've got no more stomach for slavery than you do. Here you're as free as I am.
(WILLIAMS *begins to breathe more easily. He looks around.*)

WILLIAMS
How come you live like a black man? In a slave shack?

HENRY (*Laughs.*)
Maybe to prove that *less* is *more.* You see, I'm really very wealthy; I just don't have any money, that's all.

WILLIAMS (*Still suspicious.*)
Where's your wife? An' chillun?

82

HENRY

Well, my bride is this bean patch, Mr. Williams. And I've adopted several woodchucks. And a few rather unappreciative squirrels.

WILLIAMS

Nobody "Mistered" me before—not ever.

HENRY

You better get used to it. If you're going to be a free man. You'll have to have a first name, too—oh, you don't *have* to. But it's handy.

WILLIAMS (*Tentatively.*)

Henry, maybe . . . ? Could I call myself "Mr. Henry's Williams" . . . ?

HENRY

No!

WILLIAMS (*Startled.*)

Why you shoutin' at me?

HENRY

You don't belong to anybody, sir. Except yourself. Least of all to me. Watch out—or you'll run right into what you're running away from.

WILLIAMS (*Tasting it.*)

Henry . . . Williams . . .

HENRY

If you don't like the fit of that, there's a David in my name; you can have it, I don't use it much.

WILLIAMS

I like Henry Williams! That sound good! That's a *free* man's name! (*He cups his hands and shouts.*)
HENRY WILLIAMS!

HENRY

But there's slavery in the North, too. Every man shackled to a ten-hour-a-day job is a *work*-slave. Every man who has to worry about next month's rent is a *money*-slave. Don't let that happen to you, Mr. Williams. Keep free!

WILLIAMS

I *do* feel free—here—now! With you. Never before. I hain't scared now.

HENRY

Why should you be?

WILLIAMS (*Abruptly.*)

You let me stay here? I'll work. Take my chances with the law. I'm good at hidin'! Nobody know I'm here!

HENRY

I welcome you here. But . . . you've got to find your *own* Walden, Henry Williams! Where they don't have sickening laws which keep black men in suppression. Here in Massachusetts, the color of your face is a flag. You can't hide blackness in blindness. If you want any light in your life, you'll have to find a place to live where men think of themselves as *men*—not as *white* men.

(*Putting his hand on* WILLIAMS' *shoulder.*)

Go to "Canyada"!

(*The light fades on the black man and the white man in the foreground. In the* EMERSONS' *area, the light picks up* WALDO *in the midst of an argument. His stance is twisted—almost a contortion—as if he were trying to stand simultaneously on opposite sides of a question— which he is.*)

WALDO

I have cast my vote! I've done it. I put it in the ballot-box. What more do you expect me to do?

(HENRY *moves into the scene.*)

HENRY (*Aflame with indignation.*)

Cast your whole vote. Not just a strip of paper! Your whole *influence!*

WALDO (*Turning.*)

We have to go along with the majority—!

HENRY (*Exasperated.*)

"Go along!"

WALDO (*Reasonably.*)

Henry, one must consider the economic and sociological ramifications. When white people and black try to live together, it's infinitely complicated.

HENRY (*Pounding his fist in the palm of his hand.*)

Then simplify! Simplify!

WALDO (*Shaking his head.*)

You complicate things all the more by *rushing* them. You're a naturalist, Henry. You understand the slow evolving of the seasons. It's the same with human relationships. You can't rush a sunrise.

HENRY (*With tethered anger.*)

When a man leaps from a moving freight train—and tries to scramble through the woods to cross the border into Cañada—

WALDO

Where?

HENRY (*Impatiently.*)

Into Canada! A free-er country even though they still have the Crown. But they *don't* have a Fugitive Slave Law. When a man, at the border of freedom, is stopped by the rifle of a Boston policeman, he doesn't have time for Dr. Emerson's leisurely sermon on "the slow evolving of the seasons."

WALDO

Henry, I am just as shocked at the death of this man as you are. What was his name?

HENRY (*Quietly.*)

Henry Williams. A new man. With a new name. Hardly used!

WALDO

I am just as concerned—

HENRY

Are you? To you, Henry Williams is an abstraction. You may be able to use him sometime as a digression in a Lyceum lecture.

WALDO

How can you be so unpleasant to me when I'm trying to agree with you?

(*The fever between the men is rising.*)

HENRY

I expect more from you than from anybody else; that's why I'm more disappointed in you.

WALDO

Well, *what* do you expect of me?

HENRY

Speak out!

85

WALDO

I speak.

HENRY

It's not enough. Shout!

WALDO

I am not a shouter.

HENRY

Not with your voice-box! With your brain! Waldo, *I* can't reach anybody. I can't catch the attention of people. Nobody listens to me. (*Passionately.*)

But my God, you are EMERSON!

(*There are almost tears in* HENRY's *eyes as he experiences a mixture of admiration and contempt for his idol.*)

Darling of the Lyceum, Lord of the Lecture Circuit! Every word you say from the platform is treasured, like an heirloom. Stand up, Waldo, and say what you believe!

WALDO (*Distantly.*)

Sometimes I think I invented you, Henry. Or at least prophesied you. Because you *live* what I talk about. I couldn't exist the way you do, Henry; I like my warm toast and tea and soft-boiled egg brought to me on a tray in bed each morning. Whenever I even *think* of Walden, I get a cold. But I admire you, Henry, I really do. You're my walking ethic!

(HENRY *stares at* WALDO, *marveling at how he can drift off the point.*)

Those are the exact words I used to describe you to Carlyle. Did you know that I told Carlyle about you?

HENRY (*Frustrated, turning away.*)

I don't care what you told Carlyle.

WALDO

I said to Carlyle: "Of all the men in Concord, Henry Thoreau is the best of the lot!" That's what I told him.

(*Enjoying quoting himself.*)

"A poet as full of buds of promise as a young apple tree." That's what I said.

HENRY

Waldo, don't talk *about* me—talk *to* me. Listen to me.

WALDO (*His thoughts still in England.*)
Whu—? How was that?
HENRY (*Evenly.*)
Can you lie in bed every morning? Have your breakfast brought to you
—your soft-boiled egg, your toast and tea? Can you lift your right
hand to your mouth while your left hand—which is also you—your
government—is killing men in Mexico? How can you swallow, Waldo?
How can you taste? How can you breathe? You cast your ballot with
your right hand—but has your left hand killed Henry Williams,
running to be free!
WALDO
Because I don't rant like Jeremiah, do you think I'm not outraged? I
do what *can* be done!
HENRY
That's not enough. Do the impossible. That's what you tell people in
your lectures. But you don't really believe any of it, do you? You trundle
up and down New England, stepping to the lectern with that beneficent
smile, accepting the handshake of mayors and the polite applause of
little old ladies. You go on singing your spineless benedictions.
WALDO
What I say is not spineless!
(LYDIAN *enters, drawn by their raised voices.*)
HENRY
Well, occasionally you've sounded a battle-cry. But you—you yourself
—refuse to hear it.
WALDO (*Squirming.*)
You are a very difficult man!
HENRY
Good. The world is too full of *easy* men.
WALDO
Do you want me to go out and advocate violence and rebellion?
HENRY
I ask you to *stop* violence. As for rebellion, do you think this country
was hatched from a soft-boiled egg???
(*Gesturing.*)

Look around Concord; what do you see? We have *become* everything we protested against!

WALDO

And what are you doing about it, young man? You pull the woods up over your head. You resign from the human race. Could your wood-chucks, with all their wisdom, have saved Henry Williams? Are your fish going to build roads, teach school, put out fires?

(*For a moment,* HENRY *is caught without a ready reply.*)

Oh, it's very simple for a hermit to sit off at a distance and proclaim exactly how things should be. But what if everybody did that? Where would we be?

HENRY

Where *are* we, Waldo?

WALDO

We are at war. I am aware of it.

HENRY

Are you aware of the reasons—slave-holders grasping for more slave territory? *More* slavery and less freedom, is that what you want?

WALDO

Henry, we must work within the framework of our laws. The end to this war—the condition of the blacks—this is the business of the President. And the Congress.

HENRY

Do you really believe that? Then I guess I'm wrong. I thought you had the same disgust that I have for what the military is doing. But if it doesn't trouble you, then I must've made a mistake.

(*With acid sarcasm.*)

You're right to keep still. I'll go back to the woods—and leave you at peace with your war.

(WALDO *is in genuine pain. He glances at his wife.*)

WALDO (*After a pause.*)

All right, my young conscience. What shall I do?

HENRY

Declare yourself!

(*Another pause.*)

WALDO

I will. Absolutely. The next time the occasion arises——

HENRY (*Fiercely.*)

NOW! A year ago was too late! I'll get you an audience. This afternoon. At Concord Square!

(HENRY *strides out of the light.* WALDO, *troubled, looks at* LYDIAN *in silence. The light falls away on the* EMERSONS. *A bell-rope drops from the flies as the light comes up on the thrust.* HENRY *springs up, grasps the rope, and swings on it. A bell from above peals, a reverberating command. People begin to assemble, curious and excited.*)

FARMER (*Running on.*)

Fire someplace?

WOMAN

What's the news? Is the war over?

SAM

What you doin' up there, Henry? What's goin' on?

(*There is a growing babble of voices as the crowd gathers.* HENRY *lets go of the rope as the swinging bell dies away.*)

HENRY

Dr. Emerson's coming. To speak. He's promised to make a statement! Now. Right here. Can't wait!

MOTHER (*Rushing on.*)

Oh, David Henry! Are you riling everybody up again?

HENRY

Emerson is going to rile up the whole country. And you're going to hear it *first!*

FARMER

Is he going to say something or give a sermon?

(HENRY *laughs, jubilantly.*)

HENRY

Both! God willing!

(*Others are gathering.*)

SAM

Dr. Emerson gonna speak *now?*

HENRY

I just left him! He's on his way.

(There is a babble of anticipation. One man—probably a local news-
paperman—draws out a pad and pencil, prepared to write.)

VOICE

And no lecture charge, neither!

(There is a pause as they wait. They're getting a little restless.)

WOMAN

Well, where *is* he?

(Several start to go. The reporter puts away his pad.)

HENRY *(Confidently.)*

Don't worry! He's coming. He'll be here!

(LYDIAN enters slowly, her head down. The crowd falls back to let her
through. She comes up to HENRY. Silently she looks into his face. She
clears her throat.)

LYDIAN

Dr. Emerson has asked me to tell you—

HENRY *(Gray.)*

Yes?

LYDIAN

—that he wants more time to meditate on these matters.

(HENRY does not move, merely stares at her.)

So that he can write a careful essay setting forth his position.

HENRY

And he gave his wife the happy job of coming here to tell us? Like
a walking-written-excuse to a schoolmaster, saying: "So sorry, Johnny
cannot come today, he's in bed with the croup"?

(LYDIAN shares HENRY's feeling, but her loyalty to' her husband is un-
shakable.)

LYDIAN

Waldo wants to collect his thoughts.

HENRY *(Outraged.)*

What is this, the winter of our *content*? By the time he "collects his
thoughts," they'll be dead as dandelions under the snow.

(The crowd is restless and begins to disintegrate.)

FARMER

Well, we come running to the fire, but nobody lit it. That's Henry
for ya.

90

(*As the crowd wanders off,* HENRY *stares at* LYDIAN. *Slowly, he turns away from her and starts to go, too.*)

LYDIAN (*Stopping him.*)

Henry—my husband loves you—as much as any man can love another man . . .

(HENRY *stops, but his back is still to* LYDIAN.)

HENRY (*Shaking his head.*)

My God, he was my god! No more! If he is the Deity, I am a doubter!

LYDIAN

Why do you enjoy hurting him?

HENRY (*Wheeling on her.*)

He hurts *me!*

(*They are both talking at once, their speeches overlapping.*)

LYDIAN

He cares what you think, and so he gets excited and overstates himself——

HENRY

Patronizing, that's what he is. I won't sit at the foot of his pulpit!

LYDIAN

When he talks to you——

HENRY

He never talks to me! Was he talking to me just now?

(*Bitterly.*)

He was in England, pontificating with Carlyle!

LYDIAN

You widen the distance——

HENRY

It's a waste of breath, talking to your husband. Trying to have a sane discussion with him. I lose my time, almost my identity——

LYDIAN

I hear you both. You wrangle and tussle like boys in a cricket match. Hitting and pushing and kicking each other—not for the sake of the idea, just playing to *win!*

HENRY (*Coldly.*)

Your husband, Mrs. Emerson, has the misfortune of being a gentleman. And famous. And he is drowning in his own success.

LYDIAN

My husband's best friend doesn't even know who my husband *is!* You've drawn some ideal in your mind, some imaginary Waldo—the way you want him to be. Please, Henry, give him the same liberty he gives you—to be what you are.

(HENRY *looks down, doesn't answer. Everyone has gone now.* LYDIAN *would like to say, "I'm sorry, Henry, I wish I could comfort you"— but she doesn't. Quickly,* LYDIAN *moves off.* HENRY *looks around at the empty square which was recently so full of people.*)

HENRY (*Shouts.*)

Citizens of Concord—!

(*But he is talking to the wind. Frustrated, he casts about for some way to reach the ears of a deaf public. He sees the dangling bell-rope, leaps up to ring it—and though he swings on it with the weight of his whole body, there is no sound whatsoever! THE BELL DOES NOT RING! Stunned, he pulls more frantically. Nothing.*)

How do we make a sound? How do we break the silence?

(*The light falls away on the discouraged and disheartened* HENRY. *The bell-rope vanishes in the flies. He throws himself on his cot in the cell.*

The sky goes red. HENRY *writhes on the cot. There is a cannon blast —and the sky seems ripped apart by psychedelic splatterings of shrapnel.*

A snare drum snarls a military cadence. A DRUMMER BOY *marches on, turns smartly front. The face is* EDWARD EMERSON'S. *A* SERGEANT *comes on, in the Federal uniform of the 1840's. It is* SAM STAPLES.)

SERGEANT (SAM) (*As if drilling troops.*)

Forward to Mexico . . . March!

Hate-two-three-four!

Hate-two-three-four!

Hate-two-three-four!

(*The* SERGEANT *prods* BAILEY *awake with a rifle butt.* BAILEY *staggers to attention. The* SERGEANT *puts a military cap on* BAILEY *and flings a musket into his hands. With the eternal imprecision of the civilian-soldier,* BAILEY *marches around the thrust to the insistent beat of the snare drum. The* FARMER, *uniformed, becomes part of the marching company.* BALL *appears, in a* GENERAL'S *epaulets and gold braid. He mounts the box, as if it were a military reviewing stand.*)

GENERAL (BALL) (*In the drum-cadence.*)

Learn to kill!

Learn to kill!

Learn to kill

   so you won't be killed!

(*This entire sequence has the blurred and overlapping quality of a nightmare, Goya-esque. It is a* Walpurgisnacht, *a bad trip, a sur-realistic mixing of hallucinations. Time, space, sound are wrenched awry.*)

BAILEY (*Out of the rhythm.*)

I ain't gonna shoot at them; they done nothin' to me!

(*All turn on* BAILEY.)

VARIOUS VOICES

Coward!

Slacker!

Traitor!

Deserter!

GENERAL (BALL)

Heathen!

SERGEANT (SAM)

Vagrant!

(*There is a great explosion of gunfire, and all drop to their bellies for cover. Shouts and confusion.*)

GENERAL (BALL) (*Pointing to* HENRY *on his cot.*)

Why doesn't that man have a gun?

SERGEANT (SAM) (*Shaking* HENRY's *shoulder.*)

Wake up, Henry. I got somethin' here for ya. Wake up!

HENRY

I don't want it!

(*But the* SERGEANT *forces a musket into his hands. Dazed, as if walking through syrup,* HENRY *comes to his feet. He holds the musket at arm's length distastefully.*)

GENERAL (BALL)

The purpose of this action is to stop the enemy from protecting them-selves from the enemy.

HENRY (*Helplessly defiant.*)

I won't go—!

MOTHER

That's a good boy, David Henry. Always do the right thing. Even if it's wrong.

(*The snare drum has continued, building snappishly. But* HENRY *moves arhythmically, his march out-of-sync with all the rest.*)

SERGEANT AND SOLDIERS

(*Whispered.*)

Hate-two-three-four!

Hate-two-three-four!

(*The* PRESIDENT *appears in a morning coat and striped pants. It is* WALDO.)

GENERAL (BALL)

Mr. President, the military advises that we conquer the entire territory. Level them all to rubble! Are you prepared to *go along?*

ALL VOICES

(*A kind of demonic glee.*)

Go along!

Go along!

Go along!

Go along!

(HENRY *rushes up to the* PRESIDENT. *He tries to talk, excitedly, urgently. But although his mouth is working, no sound comes out.*)

PRESIDENT (WALDO) (*Loftily, to the* GENERAL.)

Is this man saying something? I can't hear him.

(HENRY *tries to stop the other marchers, one by one; but no one pays any attention.*)

GENERAL (BALL)

What are your instructions, Mr. President?

PRESIDENT (WALDO)

I wish more time to collect my thoughts. So I am going to appoint a committee to appoint a committee to appoint a committee.

(*Cheers.*)

Get to the bottom of this, so the top will know what to do!

(*A swarthy* MEXICAN SOLDIER [WILLIAMS] *comes on with a Mexican flag.*)

SERGEANT (STAPLES)

There he is, boys, there's the enemy!

94

(*All muskets swing toward the* MEXICAN; *he is like a trapped animal.*)
HENRY (*Shouts.*)
Run, Henry Williams! Run for it!
(*The* MEXICAN SOLDIER [WILLIAMS] *leaps into the midst of the Federal troops, darts a zig-zag path among them, brandishing his banner. Rifles crack at him, shots ring wildly, the smoke continues to rise. Then* WILLIAMS *jumps off the thrust and disappears.*)
VOICE
Dirty Nigger-Spic! He got away!
HENRY (*Jubilant.*)
He's safe!
(*All of the Federal troops turn toward* HENRY *accusingly. At the same time, they realize that the drum beat has stopped. The little* DRUMMER BOY [EDWARD] *has fallen wounded across his drum.* HENRY *runs to the stricken boy, lifting him like the Pietà. Then he looks toward the statuesque* PRESIDENT [WALDO].)
HENRY
Mr. President! He only wanted to pick huckleberries!
(*The* PRESIDENT *is still benign, impervious to the confusion and the smoke.*)
PRESIDENT (WALDO)
I propose to write a careful essay, setting forth my position.
(*The rumbling of cannon and the crack of muskets continue.* HENRY *flings the musket away, then casts about, pleading to the air with his empty hands.*)
HENRY
Please! Somebody say something! Somebody speak out!
UNSEEN VOICE
Mr. Speaker. Gentlemen of the Congress!
(*Everything on stage freezes, in whatever tortured position it is, as in stopped action.* HENRY *listens with animal intentness.*)
"This unnecessary war was unconstitutionally commenced by the President, who may be telling us the Truth—but he is not telling the *Whole* Truth. He has swept the war on and on, in showers of blood. His mind, taxed beyond its powers, is running out like some tortured creature on a burning surface!"
(*With passion.*)

Stop the war, Mr. President! For the love of God, *stop this war!*
(*The figures of the battlefield begin to move again in weird, grotesque slow motion, as if mired and helpless in quicksand. But on* HENRY's *face there is a look of vast relief: someone has spoken!*)

HENRY

I do not know you, Mr. Congressman. I doubt if the people of Illinois will re-elect you, because you refused to "go along." But *I* shall remember who you are, Congressman Lincoln.
(*Deafening artillery fire peaks in volume. There are great flashes of light, the arc-ing of mortar shells, the staccato splattering of bullets. The Federal troops form into a ragged line of attacking infantrymen. They point their muskets front and move slowly forward, advancing on the audience as if it were the enemy.* HENRY *wanders, aghast at the bloodshed.*

On a bellowed command from the SERGEANT [SAM STAPLES] *all the troops drop to one knee, and raise their rifles to fire. Then we see, for the first time, in the second rank of troops a familiar face: it is* HENRY's *brother* JOHN, *in full Federal uniform. When* HENRY *sees* JOHN, *he pushes his way through the troops to run to him.*)

HENRY

John! John!
(*And just as he reaches* JOHN, *there is a fusillade of shots, a ricocheting bullet.* JOHN *is hit. He flings his arms to the sky in pain, and falls. The troops crash about in all directions, scattering to clear the area, leaving* HENRY *with the dying* JOHN *on the battlefield in the stagnant smoke. Utterly shattered,* HENRY *cradles* JOHN's *head in his arms.*)
Don't die! Not *again,* God—don't let him die!
(*The whole stage fades into darkness.*)

(*Six chimes from the bell tower. Across the sky there is the faint gray line of dawn.* BAILEY *is on his cot,* HENRY *lies in twisted, restless sleep as* SAM STAPLES—*no longer a sergeant—enters with mugs and tin plates, which he puts on the box. From now on, all are in their customary clothing.* STAPLES *shakes* HENRY's *shoulder.*)

SAM

Wake up, Henry. I got something here for ya. Wake up.

(HENRY *thrashes, still half-dreaming.*)

HENRY

I don't want it!

SAM

Well, the porridge ain't very good. But the cocoa's hot.

HENRY (*Coming painfully awake.*)

Oh. Morning, Sam. Is it morning?

SAM

Yeah. Here's yer pint of chocolate. Ya heard the news?

HENRY

What news?

SAM

It's finished.

HENRY

The war?

SAM

That wire they been stretchin' clean to Texas. And it works. Now a fella in New York can send words down there 'lectric—fast as he can talk.

HENRY

(*As he sips his chocolate thoughtfully.*)

But Sam, what if nobody in New York has anything to say to anybody in Texas?

SAM

I just thought you'd be happy to know. Another thing—uh—
(*Clearing his throat.*)
—uh—you can leave, Henry. Any time you're a mind to.

HENRY

Leave?

SAM

During the night yer tax got paid up.

HENRY

Who did it?

SAM

Hain't material fer me to say.

HENRY

Waldo! Did Dr. Emerson pay it?

SAM

No sir.

HENRY

My mother.

SAM

No.

HENRY

Did you?

SAM

I offered, Henry. You flat refused.

HENRY

Mrs. Emerson. Did she come and pay it?

SAM

Now stop pokin' around tryin' to get me to tell. I promised your Aunt
Louisa I wouldn't open my——

HENRY (*Disgusted.*)

Aunt Louisa!

(BAILEY *is beginning to stir.*)

I am cursed with the charity of my mother's sister!

(*Shouting offstage to her.*)

Aunt Louisa, why couldn't you leave your nose and your false teeth
out of my life! I hereby EXCOMMUNICATE YOU FROM THE
MILKY WAY!

(SAM *swings the jail door open, hands* HENRY *a paper.*)

SAM

Been nice havin' ya with us, Henry. Here's the receipt.

(HENRY *ignores the paper.*)

HENRY

I don't want it. You can't accuse *me* of paying my tax!

SAM

It's been paid!

HENRY

Not by me. I'm still guilty.

(HENRY *sits on the cot, doggedly.*)

98

SAM

Henry, a man's got no right to stay in jail if they's no charge ag'in him. I can't even bring you lunch.

BAILEY (*A bit wistfully.*)

You goin' already?

SAM

He's goin'!

HENRY

No!

SAM

Law put you in here. The law says when you're out.

BAILEY

Gonna be God-a'mighty quiet around here . . .

(HENRY *stares intensely at* BAILEY.)

What's wrong?

HENRY (*Softly.*)

Everything's wrong—when a man only thinks about himself.

(*Wheeling sharply on* SAM.)

Sam! You know what *quid pro quo* means?

SAM (*Pained.*)

That one of them Harvard words?

HENRY

It means if you see to it that Bailey gets his trial—not in another three months, or another three weeks, but *now,* right away—why, then maybe I'll favor your law by walking out onto the sidewalk. Not before.

SAM

It ain't in my power. I don't make decisions like that.

(HENRY *gets back into his cot, pulls the blanket over him.*)

HENRY

Goodnight, Sam.

SAM (*Suffering.*)

It's *morning,* Henry.

HENRY

Not for me. Not until you let Bailey out.

SAM

I'll do everything I kin. I'll talk to the Judge and the Selectmen.

HENRY

Tell them unless Mr. Bailey's trial is right away, they'll have another eating, non-paying guest in their jail——permanently!

(SAM *goes out, almost wishing he were a soldier in Mexico.* BAILEY *is moved. Nobody in his life has ever stood up for him like this.*)

BAILEY

Thankee. I ain't ever gonna fergit this night here. And—when I'm out —I'm gonna come visit you, if you don't mind—at your pond place.

(*The sound of the flute re-enters, but there is no leafy projection— only the mounting flames of dawn. Pause:* HENRY *is making a difficult decision. He comes down, staring far off, toward Walden.*)

HENRY

I may not be there at the "pond place," Bailey. Seems to me I've got several more lives to live. And I don't know if I can spare any more time for *that* one.

BAILEY

Sounds to me like it's just about perfick.

HENRY

That's the trouble. If I live there much longer, I might live there forever. And you have to think twice before you accept heaven on terms like that.

(*Abruptly.*)

You ever take a boat trip, Bailey?

BAILEY

Riverboat only.

HENRY

When you buy a cabin ticket for an ocean passage, they give you the liberty of the whole ship. It's a privilege that should be *used*. Man shouldn't stay the whole voyage just in one place, below decks, no matter how dry and cozy it is. And warm.

(*Simply.*)

I think I'll have to roam the whole ship. Go before the mast! Stand out there on the foredeck.

(*The flute melody falls away.*)

Bailey, I tried to escape. But escape is like sleep. And when sleep is permanent, it's death.

(*A pause. He moves closer to the imagined downstage window, so the morning sun fills his face.*)

I must leave Walden.

(*The words are painful to him.* BAILEY *goes toward* HENRY *as if to comfort him, raising a hand toward his shoulder; but* BAILEY *is helpless.*)

It's not necessary to be there in order to *be* there.

(BAILEY *moves to the window, prompted by the growing light on* HENRY's *face. He looks out, awed.*)

BAILEY

Bright morning. Gonna be a fine July day out there.

HENRY

Sometimes the light gets so bright it puts your eyes out. And then it's just darkness all over again.

(*He looks up. The sky is really brilliant with the sunlight now.*)

But there is more day to dawn. The sun is only a morning star.

(*He shakes hands with* BAILEY, *starts out, remembers something: his shoe. He gets it from under the bed, salutes* BAILEY *with it.*

In the doorway, HENRY *stops, looks up sharply.*

From a distance, he hears an eccentric, non-military drummer.

He moves into Concord Square ablaze with morning light. Suddenly the drumbeat comes from a different direction, growing in volume. It is like thunder all around him.

His eyes follow the arc of the sky. He seems to grow in stature, lifted and strengthened by a greater challenge.

He waves to BAILEY, *who waves back warmly from the cell window.*

With determinaiton, HENRY *leaps from the stage and strides up the aisle of the theatre to the sound of his own different drummer.*

No curtain falls. The lights do not fade, but grow brighter. During the curtain calls, and as the audience leaves the theatre, HENRY's *distinctive and irregular drum-cadence builds and resounds.*)

Production Notes from the Playwrights

Thoreau's decision to return to the human race is the shape, the parabola of the play: his evolution from withdrawal to return, the journey from hermitizing to social conscience. This is the subtext of the play; the director and the actor must evolve it surely, slowly, so it is like the opening of a flower.

His night in jail is a mystical experience for this highly sensitive man. Confined, he has the liberty to explore what he really *is*, the composite of his experiences, past and *future*. It is an ecstasy, a "passion," a revelation, a summing up of his life in the curve of time from sunset to sunrise.

This is not the bearded, weary-eyed Thoreau of the recent postage-stamp. This is a blazing contemporary, clean-shaven, vigorous, outraged at the insanity and inanity of civilization around him. The purpose of the play is to go deeper than the words he wrote, to probe the turmoil out of which he wrote them.

If he was a revolutionary, it was in the spirit of those who, fourscore years before him, had imagined a United States—where the conserving of established order was less sacred than the hopeful helix of *change*. In the course of his night in jail, Thoreau realizes that the idyll of Walden has already worked its change upon him; and the sunrise goads him with new challenges.

For your production style, be guided by Thoreau's own advice: "Simplify!" The more you can omit physically, the more your audience will be called on to contribute in imagination. This play is more than the ruminating of one man in one place in one night. We are not tied down to "flashback" or reminiscence. All the people of the play, including the audience, should be encouraged to partake in a banquet of imagining. It is eminently Thoreauvian that everyone should bring to —and take from—the play something uniquely his own.

J. L. and R. E. L.